THE CHANNEL ISLANDS

To Marion, with whom I discovered the Channel Islands

*   *   *

Contents

Acknowledgements

My thanks are due to the States of Jersey Tourism Committee and to the Guernsey Tourist Office for all their help and hospitality during the writing of this book. Vital information, assistance and facilities were also provided by British Airways, British Island Airways, Aurigny Air Services, British Rail (Sealink), Modernline Travel, the Modernline Hotels Group, the Jersey Wildlife preservation Trust, and by the following individuals: Michael Beaumont, Raymond Falla, Jimmy Janes, A. H. S. ('Sam') Lucas, Drew and Sybil McQueen, Jeremy Mallinson, Len Matchan, Marion Mead, Bill and Dawn Nunn, Ray Parkin, John Possnicker, H. T. J. Ozanne, Leslie Rebindaine, Michael Walden, Ann Walker, and Peter and Jenny Wood.

The Author and Publishers would like to thank the following for their permission to reproduce the illustrations in this book: Peter Baker International Picture Library for nos 12, 13, 20, 21, 22 and 23; Mr. Anthony Kersting for nos 1, 2, 3, 4, 5, 9, 10, 11, 14, 15, 16, 17 and 18; The Tate Gallery, London, for no. 6; and the John Topham Picture Library for nos 7, 8, and 19. The maps of Jersey and St. Helier are reproduced by permission of the States of Jersey Tourism Committee, and all the other maps by permission of the Guernsey Tourist Office.

List of Illustrations

ONE

Introducing the Channel Islands

Geographically, the Channel Islands—Jersey, Guernsey, Alderney, Sark, Herm, Jethou, and a smattering of islets— are undoubtedly part of France. They lie between 60 and 100 miles south of the British mainland in the inverted 'L' formed by the coasts of Normandy and Brittany, and in clear weather the French coast, as little as eight miles away, is clearly visible. But historically speaking the islands are a part of Britain, for they were part of Normandy when William the Conqueror invaded England in 1066, beat Harold at the Battle of Hastings, and assumed the English Crown. Thus mainland Britain and the Channel Islands became linked—and islanders point out that as they remained true to the British Crown when Normandy broke away in 1204 they can, strictly speaking, claim Britain as a 'possession'.

For their loyalty to the British Crown, the Channel Islands were promised by King John 'the continuance of their ancient laws and privileges'—privileges which allow them to be self-governing. As a result of this, the islands make their own laws, fix their own taxes and have no representatives in the British Parliament at Westminster. Yet they owe allegiance to the Queen, and the British Government is responsible for the islands' external affairs such as foreign policy and defence. Jersey and Guernsey have their own banknotes, coinage and postage stamps, yet British currency is accepted, habits and food are much the same as in Britain and familiar British chain stores and banks line the main shopping streets. There are no entry formalities for British visitors (you do not even need a passport), and traffic drives on the left. But the French connection remains strong. Although everybody speaks English, the official language is French. Many of the street names are in French, and the islands' leading families often have French names too. The names of bays and beauty spots often have a Continental ring about them, and in recent years links with France have been strengthened by a direct hydrofoil service from St. Malo to Jersey which has brought about a huge increase in the number of visitors from the Continent. Continental cuisine has also been introduced to the islands by French and other European hoteliers who have started businesses there.

This mixed Anglo-French identity, coupled with the islands' enviable weather record, has helped to create and maintain the islands' image as a popular holiday centre. Between the wars both Jersey and Guernsey built up big tourist industries based on the steamer service from Southampton, then up to ten hours' journey away. The islands suffered what could have been a major setback during the Second World War when they were occupied by the Germans. The occupying forces made many structural alterations and built defensive strong-points on the islands which remain to this day. But after the war the islands quickly recovered their position, aided by faster ferry services from Weymouth and almost hourly flights from London to Jersey and Guernsey. Today, British visitors can reach the Channel Islands in as little as 25 minutes on a direct jet flight, and Jersey in particular has built up a reputation as a 'swinging' spot. Part of the attraction is undoubtedly that holidaymakers feel that in visiting Jersey, Guernsey, or one of their smaller neighbours, they are in a way 'going abroad'.

This impression is fostered by the islands' sunshine record, with one or other of them regularly topping the unofficial sunshine league of British resorts. Just which island is the sunniest is a matter of dispute between Jersey and Guernsey, who both maintain meteorological stations. Jersey, the largest and most southerly of the islands, is a natural suntrap for it is tilted towards the south. But in recent years it is Guernsey which has often claimed those few vital extra hours of sunshine which make all the difference between winning and losing the 'sunshine league', and Jerseymen can be heard muttering darkly that this is because Guernsey has moved its weather station to the low-lying and relatively mist-free L'Ancresse Common.

Be that as it may, nature obviously believes that Jersey is the mildest of the islands. Sub-tropical trees like the palm and eucalyptus flourish there; spring daffodils clothe the cliffs very early in the year while the other islands still boast nothing more colourful than decaying bracken; the Jersey Orchid grows there alone in the British Isles; the California tree lupin decorates the sand-dunes in summer; even the granite walls are home to a flower: the tiny Mexican Fleabane daisy; and at Christmas the crimson camellia is still a blaze of colour. For these and other blessings Jersey must thank the Gulf Stream, the waters of which bring a hint of Caribbean warmth to the sea around the Channel Islands and exert a beneficial influence upon the climate. Winters are mild, frosts are rare, and although it may snow, there is usually a thaw within a matter of hours.

The feeling of being 'abroad' is also encouraged by prices in the shops, for these are certainly nothing like those on the mainland. The islands fix their own rates of taxation and have no V.A.T. As a result wine, spirits, liqueurs, cigarettes, cigars, tobacco, perfume, toiletries, cameras, tape recorders and many other luxury goods are all far cheaper than elsewhere. Local rates of taxation vary, but overall Guernsey is probably the cheapest island for shoppers.

Although they have thriving tourist industries, the Channel Islands are still largely dependent upon agriculture for their living—it is the second largest industry in Jersey and the largest in Guernsey. The emphasis is on early potatoes, tomatoes, flowers such as carnations grown under glass, and the famous Channel Islands breeds of cattle—Jerseys, Guernseys and Alderneys (other breeds are usually barred on the islands). Jersey also cultivates an oddity in the shape of a giant cabbage, the stalk of which is long enough to turn into a walking stick which makes an unusual souvenir. The extra hours of sunshine are often claimed to be responsible for the islands' fine farm produce.

Besides agriculture and tourism, the islands have of late made a breakthrough into the commercial world because of the tax advantages which businesses may enjoy from being registered there. Banks and merchant banks now abound in Jersey and

Guernsey, and even the doorways of tiny St. Anne, the capital of Alderney, are beginning to be studded with the little brass plates which proclaim that a particular firm has its registered offices there. Tax advantages have attracted new light industries to the islands too, to the benefit of their balance of payments. But although industry may stay, the days of the banks and merchant banks may be numbered. The islands are now part of the European Economic Community, and there are doubts as to whether the tax advantages will always remain in force.

Despite the fact that they have managed to move with the times, and despite the fact that they are visited by so many holidaymakers every year, the islands remain remarkably unspoiled. Jersey, dismissed by many of those who have never been there as a 'commercialised resort', is nothing of the sort. Although it is a lively entertainment centre with some superb hotels, it has plenty of quiet wooded valleys, green fields and rolling farmland as well. The island has an area of about 45 square miles, much of it fields. The north coast is made up of high cliffs, excellent for walking, and the island slopes gently down to the sheltered bays and sandy beaches on the south coast around the capital and port of St. Helier. Together with some rocky islets to the south, it comprises the States of Jersey.

Guernsey, 20 miles north of Jersey, is the second largest island and is more or less at the centre of the group. It is triangular in shape, and the predominant cliffs on the south coast mean that the island is 'tilted' to the north. But the flat northern tip of the island nevertheless enjoys exceptionally clear weather, while the sheltered bays in the south are usually protected from the wind. The main town, St. Peter Port, is built on a hillside and is the most attractive in the Channel Islands. It has views across to the neighbouring islands of Herm, Sark and Jethou. Guernsey is quieter and less sophisticated than its southern neighbour, and in many ways it is scenically more attractive. But it has large acreages under glass, and this sometimes gives one the impression of being on a giant small-holding. With all the other islands except Jersey, it comprises the self-governing States of Guernsey.

Feudal Sark, nine miles east of Guernsey, is a possible excursion venue as well as a centre for away-from-it-all holidays which really are away from it all. It is famous for its dramatic cliff scenery, as well as for the fact that its ruling Seigneur bans all cars and aircraft from the island.

Alderney, 20 miles north of Guernsey and only eight miles from the French coast, is perhaps the least known of the Channel Islands. It is a rather ugly island which has suffered through the years from being strategically important to anyone wishing to control the Channel. It is dominated by the huge harbour, built during a British attempt to turn it into the 'Gibraltar' of the Channel, and by the ruins of the Napoleonic forts ringing its coast. During the Second World War, Alderney's entire population was evacuated before its occupation by the Germans, and the Germans added to its ugliness by using slave labour to build even more fortifications. After the war there was talk of developing it into a sort of huge holiday camp, but it escaped this fate and now consists of the attractive and centrally situated little town of St. Anne, a tiny airport, and some practically deserted beaches. For visitors there is nothing to do except walk, sunbathe, sleep and eat, and they will receive a mixed welcome from a small population made up almost entirely of British expatriates. Alderney now is the only financial provisions which apply on the other islands. without coming across the complicated laws and stringent financial provisions which still apply on the other islands.

About three miles off the coast of Guernsey are the other two islands, Herm and Jethou. Both are privately leased and Jethou, a small conical shaped island, cannot be visited without special permission. But Herm, one and a half miles long and half a mile wide, attracts thousands of day trippers every year as well as the guests who stay at its one hotel. With its fine cliffs, sheltered bays and famous Shell Beach, where the Gulf Stream deposits shells from as far away as the Caribbean, it is everybody's dream island.

Alderney people excepted, the islanders have a character of their own and doubtless one which has been forged both by history and by the surroundings in which they live. They have the unhurried, contemplative air which holidaymakers always find so catching; and their eyes have the far-away look of those whose horizons are always bounded by the sea. But they also have a wry sense of humour and, with their high standard of living, their tastes can be sophisticated. In winter, when the tourist trade falls off, the restaurants serving good food and fine wines are still crowded, a fact which may lie behind but somehow contradicts the islanders' claim that they have nothing to do all winter except drink and commit adultery. Jerseymen will jokingly describe their island as '70,000 alcoholics clinging to a rock', and Alderney frequently says that its only export is empty bottles. In fact, the islanders' tastes are far more highly developed than that, and many of their homes display an exciting inno-vatory streak.

There is change, of course, and sadly some of the old things are disappearing. For example: the Norman-French patois used in Guernsey, Jersey and Alderney. This patois is one of the peculiarities of the Channel Islands. You can still hear it spoken in country districts and in the markets, and although it differs from island to island the various dialects are understood by all patois speakers. But because the patois is not taught in schools, it is a dying language—although there are hopes that the Jersey and Guernsey versions of the patois may well be saved.

Other island traditions are alive and kicking, and an example of this is the legal oddity dating from the Norman period and known as the 'Clameur de Haro'. An islander who feels that he is being legally wronged in the form of a trespass on or against property can invoke the Clameur by falling to his knees in the presence of witnesses and crying 'Haro! Haro! Haro! à l'aide, mon Prince, on me fait tort' (Help, my Prince, they are wronging me). This action, thought to be an appeal to the Viking leader Rollo, was constituted in the tenth century, and has the same effect as an injunction. It is a practice which invokes mirth out-side the islands, but in fact anyone ignoring the Clameur does so at his peril, for heavy fines are still imposed if the action which is being complained of does not cease immediately until the matter can be decided in court. Practical jokers should be warned that invoking the Clameur needlessly also carries a heavy penalty.

Other island oddities include the ormer—a shellfish unique to the Channel Islands with a particularly attractive shell like mother of pearl and which is a delicacy much enjoyed by the islanders although the uninitiated may draw an unkind comparison between eating an ormer and chewing a particularly salty car tyre—and the heavy-knit sweaters known as 'jerseys' and 'guernseys' which have given their names to knitwear all over the world. Jerseys and guernseys are both crew-necked fishermen's sweaters made of oiled wool and knitted to a traditional pattern in navy blue or white. Nowadays, the guernsey is the most popular of these and it can be bought in almost any colour; the jersey is similar to a guernsey but has an anchor pattern on the front.

In an attempt to boost their tourist trade, Jersey and Guernsey have both made strenuous efforts to extend their tourist seasons. Both offer cut-price winter package holidays to major hotels, and there is all-year-round entertainment. This trend is likely to continue because, as the islanders point out, they do have a climate similar to that of Bermuda. But while this is true of the summer months it is fair to say that because the islands are exposed to the Atlantic the water is colder than one might expect and swimming is comfortable only between June and late September. The islands are also subject to dense sea mists which can disrupt air traffic. Such disadvantages might be outweighed by the exceptionally clear air which means that it is always important to guard against unexpected sunburn.

Jersey has led the way in introducing new attractions such as a spring festival and a gastronomic festival. But the most popular carnival on both Jersey and Guernsey is one which they share with the South of France: the annual Battle of Flowers. These picturesque events, involving a procession of floats beautifully decorated with flowers, take place on both islands in August and are a high spot of any holiday.

Apart from these annual carnivals, and the few traditions and superstitions connected with individual islands, the Channel Islands seem to lack a folklore of their own. Although the islands have produced their fair share—perhaps more than their fair share—of historical figures, among them many overseas explorers, they do not seem to have a great deal in the way of their own literature, or even music. No folk music has survived the

Reformation, and the various island museums offer few clues as to how the people passed the long winter evenings.

Perhaps they spent it in plotting, dreaming, and politicising— for the islands certainly seem to have produced some of history's more extrovert characters. The Jersey Royalist, Sir George Carteret, left his stamp upon the Civil War. Guernseyman Thomas de la Rue, a printer's apprentice, was a giant of the newspaper and publishing world in England as well as founding the stationery business which still bears his name today. Major General Sir Isaac Brock, a Guernseyman, died at the Battle of Queenston Heights in 1812, saving Upper Canada from the Americans.

A Guernseyman, Sir John Everett Millais, whose family came from Jersey, was one of Britain's most famous artists during the nineteenth century and became President of the Royal Academy. Sir Seymour Hicks, the famous actor, comedian, and theatrical producer who died in 1949, was a Jersey man. So was the play-wright and librettist Frederick Lonsdale, the man who wrote *On Approval* and *Maid of the Mountains.* Jerseywomen have also left their mark on the literary scene, led by novelist Elinor Glyn.

And, of course, the most famous Jerseywoman of them all was Lillie Langtry, the actress, who caught the eye of Edward VII while he was still Prince of Wales. Lillie Langtry, a rector's daughter, was born in St. Saviour's in 1853, and was twice married. Her nickname stemmed from a Millais portrait of her holding a lily which he called 'a Jersey Lily'. Millais described Lillie Langtry as 'quite simply the most beautiful woman on earth'. That certainly seems to have been Prince Edward's view of her for their association at the turn of the century caused a world-wide scandal. Lillie Langtry died in 1929, and is buried in St. Saviour's churchyard, Jersey.

But, as befits a group of islands surrounded by dangerous seas and washed by some of Europe's highest tides, the islands' most famous sons are their naval heroes. Among them is Philip de Carteret, from Jersey, who was on the South Pacific exploration voyage which annexed the Falkland Islands for Britain, and who later commanded the ship which discovered Pitcairn Island in 1767 and made a number of other discoveries on his way to the Philippines and the Dutch West Indies. His compatriot, Sir Charles Le Hardy, a naval captain, was second in command of the Channel Fleet, and was Governor of New York in 1755. And Lord de Saumarez, a naval lieutenant who served on Nelson's *Victory*, went on to become a vice-admiral and, later, a General of Marines. As a captain, the then Sir James de Saumarez, had something of a naval victory by leading a British squadron through very dangerous waters off Guernsey in order to escape from a superior French force. Asked how he had completed such a manoeuvre and what he had used for markers, de Saumarez pointed to the shore and retorted: 'Yonder is my house'.

Today's occupants of the Channel Islands are less heroic, but often equally famous. They include the Earl of Shrewsbury, premier earl of Britain; holiday camp king Sir Billy Butlin; zoologist and author Gerald Durrell; golfer Tony Jacklin; boxer Billy Walker; TV personality Alan Whicker; Sir William Haley, a former editor of *The Times*; banker Sir Julian Hodge; painter Sir Francis Cook; naval architect E. H. Buchanan; entertainer Ronnie Ronalde; and author Jack Higgins.

TWO

History

The history of the Channel Islands goes back at least 100,000 years to when Palaeolithic men are known to have occupied cave dwellings on the islands, the most famous of these being La Cotte de St. Brelade on Jersey. Climatic changes then led to the islands being deserted for a long period and it was 50,000 years later, during the last Ice Age, that Neanderthal man moved back to the islands. Thirteen teeth from Neanderthal man, found on Jersey, can be seen in the museum at St. Helier.

But the first people really to leave their mark on the islands were the Neolithic men in 4000 to 3000 BC. Their most notable monuments are their large stone tombs or dolmens; there are seven of these on Jersey of which the most famous is La Hougue Bie in Grouville, about three miles from St. Helier, which is still covered by its original 40-feet mound of earth and is one of the finest prehistoric tombs in Europe. Visitors can clamber along the low, 33-feet-long passage, roofed with huge stones, which leads inside to the great chamber and three side cells. The air strikes cold inside whatever the season, and in fact the temperature inside the tomb never varies. Radio carbon dating has established the construction date as being between 3000 and 2500 BC.

The quieter and less dramatic Faldouet Dolmen can also be seen in a field about a mile away. In Jersey there is also a hidden prehistoric forest at St. Ouen's Bay where, at very low tides, submerged tree trunks are occasionally exposed by the shifting sands — evidence that Jersey once stretched farther west than it does now. On Guernsey, the finest dolmen is the Déhus Dolmen near Bordeaux Harbour which has been recently restored. The central chamber is about 17 feet by 14 feet and there are three side chambers with narrow openings. There are two other easily accessible dolmens — Druid's Altar, and the 33-feet-long La Varde Dolmen — on L'Ancresse Common.

The Roman occupation of France in the first century BC resulted in an influx of Gauls to the Channel Islands. There are very few Roman remains on the islands, although many Roman coins have been found, and it is thought that there was no regular Roman occupation. The Emperor Antoninus is said to have called Jersey 'Caesarea', Guernsey 'Sarnia', and Alderney 'Riduna' — names with which the islands and their transport services still toy. As Roman influence waned, the islands are unlikely to have been permanently settled because of the risk from raiders: Saxon and Frisian freebooters, the Vandals and finally the Vikings, who swept down from Scandinavia in their long boats in the ninth century.

One of these Vikings, a Christian named Rollo, became the first Duke of Normandy in 911 when the north-west corner of France was ceded to them by King Charles 'the Simple' of France. The Clameur de Haro is thought to originate from these times — with 'Haro' really being an abbreviation of 'Ha, Rollo!' — an appeal to Rollo for help.

Rollo's son, William Longsword, added the Channel Islands to the Duchy of Normandy in about 933. As a result there were undoubtedly some islanders in the Norman force which under William II, seventh Duke of Normandy and known as William the Conqueror, defeated the English at the Battle of Hastings on 14 October 1066. Since that time the Channel Islands have, with the exception of a few short breaks, been associated with the crown of England, and are the oldest part of the British Commonwealth.

In 1204 the French, under King Philip II, recaptured Normandy, but the Channel Islands remained faithful to King John. Whether this was due to a sense of loyalty, or to the fact that King John had taken the precaution of holding members of the islands' leading families as hostages, is not certain — but King John is thought to have visited the islands in 1213 and he certainly granted the islanders 'continuance of their ancient laws and

privileges'—privileges which form the basis of the islands' constitution and their self-governing status. These privileges were
confirmed by King Henry III who visited Jersey in 1230. In 1279
King Edward I granted the islands a Public Seal, bearing the Royal
Arms (three leopards), and in 1290 separate Bailiffs were
appointed for Jersey and Guernsey. Today the Bailiff, a Crown
appointment, still presides over the Parliament and courts of
both the States of Jersey and the States of Guernsey.

During the fourteenth century the first of the islands' castles
were built—at Cornet in Guernsey and at Grosnez and Gorey in
Jersey—as French threats to repossess the islands increased. The
formation of the Jersey Militia and Guernsey Militia also dates
from this period. The French invaded the Channel Islands twice
in 1338 and occupied Castle Cornet on Guernsey. In 1339 Mont
Orgueil Castle, built on a promontory at Gorey and dominating
Jersey's east coast, was also attacked but unsuccessfully. Castle
Cornet was recaptured by English forces in 1345, but in 1356 it
was again captured by the French although they held it for only
a few months. Eventually the French abandoned all claims to the
Channel Islands under the Treaty of Calais in 1360.

At about this time the Fishermen's Chapel, in St. Brelade's,
Jersey, parts of which are said to date from the sixth century, had
its stone roof raised and its frescoes appear to have been executed
by the monks. Beside the chapel one can still see the old 'perquage'
or sanctuary, path leading to the sea: until the Reformation all
Jersey's churches had these paths, which enabled criminals taking
sanctuary in the churches to escape the often harsh justice of the
times by fleeing from the island. Anyone leaving in this way had
all his goods confiscated and was barred from returning to the
island—but he could not be physically harmed in the church or
on the 24-feet-wide perquage path.

In 1461 the French captured Jersey, with Gorey Castle falling
to the invaders through the Governor's treachery rather than due
to any military force. The resulting occupation of the island lasted
only until 1468, but it is thought that it was during this period
that Grosnez Castle, in the north-west of Jersey, was destroyed.

A more peaceful period for the islands began in March 1483
when Pope Sixtus IV issued a Bull ordering that the islands and

their surrounding waters should be treated as neutral in time of war and that enemy ships and goods should be immune from capture within this area. Although there were occasional breaches of the order, despite the threat of excommunication, the islands turned this period of peace to good advantage by building up their reputation as trading centres. The Bull remained in force until 1689. Elizabeth Castle was built in St. Aubin's Bay, off St. Helier, between 1590 and 1600, and was named by Sir Walter Raleigh, then Governor of the island, in honour of Queen Elizabeth I.

Both Mont Orgueil Castle and Elizabeth Castle featured strongly in the Civil War, when Charles I sent his son, the young Prince of Wales, to take refuge in Jersey, a Royalist stronghold, for 10 weeks (17 April to 25 June 1646); and when news reached the island that King Charles I had been beheaded in 1649, Jersey was the first place to recognize Charles II as King. The proclamation was made in the Royal Square of St. Helier and the original document is preserved in the museum. James, Duke of York (later King James II) also found refuge in Jersey from 17 September 1649 to 13 February 1650. Meanwhile, Guernsey had declared for Parliament, so the islands found themselves on opposite sides in the war.

After the King's defeat by Cromwell, Jersey's loyalty to the Crown made it the object of Parliamentarian anger, and in 1651 an expedition under Admiral Robert Blake landed at St. Ouen's Bay and Jersey Royalist forces under Sir George Carteret withdrew to Elizabeth Castle. Parliamentary forces quickly captured the neighbouring St. Aubin's Fort, and Gorey Castle also surrendered within a few days. But Elizabeth Castle withstood siege for 50 days before capitulating, and the garrison was permitted to march out on honourable terms. On Guernsey Castle Cornet, which had alone remained loyal to the King, suffered a far longer siege of eight years and nine months. But this too was broken in December 1651, and the garrison were accorded the honours of war. Cromwell was lenient towards Jersey's Royalists, returning their properties on generous terms. King Charles II returned to England in 1660 and within a week was once again proclaimed King in St. Helier's Royal Square. Sir George Carteret and the other Jersey Royalists were generously rewarded for their loyalty, and New Jersey in the United States takes its name from Jersey because in 1664 Sir George Carteret became joint proprietor of the land which now comprises that state, having been introduced to the area when the King gave him some islands off the coast of Virginia.

During the seventeenth century many of the fine manor houses in the Channel Islands were constructed and in the latter half of the eighteenth century the Martello towers, which dominate many of the bays on both Jersey and Guernsey, were built as beach defences against a renewed French threat. The towers differ slightly on the two islands. The precaution of building these defences proved to be a wise one, for in 1781 the French did invade Jersey after an unsuccessful attempt two years earlier, and Baron de Rullecourt landed at La Rocque and reached St. Helier. The Lieutenant Governor was surprised by the invaders in bed at his home, and signed a surrender document. But the island's military commander, Major Francis Peirson, ignored the surrender order and led the Militia and two regiments stationed on the island into action against the invaders in Royal Square. The French were defeated, but both Peirson and de Rullecourt were killed in the battle and are buried in the parish church.

After this scare, it was decided to build Fort Regent on the granite hill overlooking St. Helier. The fort was completed in 1814, but never saw action. The Battle of Waterloo in 1815 resulted in the end of military action between England and France.

The period following the Napoleonic Wars was one of increasing prosperity for the Channel Islands. During the First World War islanders served with distinction in the British forces, but Guernsey suffered a tragedy when 600 men from the Royal Guernsey Light Infantry were killed in two days at Cambrai in November 1917. Castle Cornet was used as a French seaplane base, and a large camp for German prisoners of war was built on Jersey.

In the years between the wars, improved sea communications strengthened the commercial ties with Britain, and Guernsey and Jersey began to develop tourist industries. These received a boost in 1933 when regular land-based air services to the islands began. There had been experimental flights with flying boats as early as

1923, and in 1924 a weekly flying boat service was introduced by Imperial Airways between Southampton and Guernsey (fare: £5.50 return). This service continued until 1929. In 1933 the first land-based service began between Portsmouth and Jersey. Flying time was one and a quarter hours and the return fare was £2.75. The aircraft, carrying eight passengers, had to use the beach at St. Aubins Bay for landing until Jersey Airport, at St. Peter, was opened in 1933. Guernsey did not enjoy regular air services until much later, due to a ban on civil aviation and a dispute about the siting of their airport.

THREE

The German Occupation

The most dramatic period in the history of the Channel Islands began at the end of June 1940 when the islands, which were considered by the British Government to be indefensible, were declared a demilitarized zone and thus put at the mercy of the German forces which had just overrun France. The islands soon became the only part of the British Isles to be occupied by the Germans, and they endured five dreary years of deprivation during which all the inhabitants except the native islanders were eventually deported. Alderney was entirely depopulated and turned into a slave camp, and Jersey and Guernsey became German fortresses bristling with gun emplacements and observation posts. The Germans prepared to defend to the last those very islands which Britain considered to be indefensible.

The story of this virtual handing over of the islands to the Germans is one of confusion. Britain seemed to have turned her back on the islands right from the outset of the war. Both the Guernsey Militia and the Jersey Militia were loyally called up for action on the day war broke out—four days before they received official British approval for this action.

On the islands, precautionary measures in the period between the Munich crisis and the outbreak of war had been characteristically vague and of dubious usefulness. It had been decided, for example, that all homing pigeons in Jersey should be notified to the authorities and that Constables shoud be authorised to take possession of any sand in their parishes for making sandbags, despite the fact that sand is the one commodity in which Jersey abounds.

The British Government had, in fact, long decided that the Channel Islands had virtually no strategic value, were wide open to attack from France by sea and air, and were impossible to defend because of the risk to the inhabitants. The battalion of regular British troops stationed in Jersey was withdrawn in 1925, and the battalion in Guernsey was hastily pulled out in 1939.

But the Channel Islands were pugnaciously loyal. The realisation that they were being abandoned to their fate hit the people of Alderney first. In the middle of June 1940 British troops on Alderney were suddenly evacuated without explanation. The island's Chief Administrator, Judge French, had to call a meeting of all the islanders to reassure them that the troops were merely being moved to Jersey and Guernsey — but the implication that Alderney, the closest of the islands to the French coast, was being abandoned to its fate, was obvious. Morale was lowered even farther when French troops, fleeing from occupied France, arrived in Alderney in a state of exhaustion. The British evacuation was completed with almost indecent speed, and large amounts of military equipment were left behind on the quayside. It was the inhabitants of Alderney who volunteered to dispose of these military goods as well as remaining stocks of petrol and diesel oil on the island.

Churchill was against giving up the islands without a fight. But the Navy pointed out that a seaborne invasion of the islands could not be prevented because of their proximity to the French coast and the distance from Britain. On 19 June it was announced that the U.K. Government had decided to demilitarize the islands, which meant the demobilisation of the militia and the surrender of uniforms, arms and equipment. Remaining British troops were rapidly evacuated.

On 24 June the Bailiffs of Jersey and Guernsey received the following message from the King: 'For strategic reasons it has been found necessary to withdraw the armed forces from the Channel Islands. I deeply regret this necessity and I wish to assure my people in the Islands that in taking this decision my Government has not been unmindful of their position. It is in their interest that this step should be taken in present circumstances. The long association of the Islands with the Crown and the loyal service the people of the Islands have rendered to my ancestors and myself are guarantees that the link between us will remain unbroken and I know that my people in the Islands will look forward with the same confidence as I do to the day when the resolute fortitude with which we face our present difficulties will reap the reward of victory.'

But, through either reluctance or inefficiency, the British Government did not convey to the Germans their decision to demilitarize the islands until 30 June, when the United States Ambassador in London was asked to transmit a message to Germany announcing that 'the evacuation of all military personnel and equipment from the Channel Islands was completed some days ago. The islands are, therefore, demilitarized and cannot be considered in any way as a legitimate target for bombardment.' The message came two days too late. On 28 June the Germans attacked St. Peter Port, just after a public meeting in the streets and while the mail boat *Isle of Sark* was in the harbour. Thirty-three people were killed and more than thirty wounded by bombs and machine-gun bullets, with the only resistance coming from anti-aircraft guns on the *Isle of Sark*. A similar attack on St. Helier killed eleven people and injured nine.

On 30 June airborne troops occupied Guernsey, using the new airport at Forest, and the next day Jersey too was invaded. For the Germans this moment of setting foot on British soil was one of great pride. The German troops who spearheaded the invasion were told, inaccurately, that they were the first to land on British soil in the history of modern warfare—and many of them firmly believed that they were on the Isle of Wight.

Meanwhile, ships had been provided during the previous fortnight to evacuate those islanders who wished to leave and particularly those, such as men of military age, who would have been put in danger by remaining on the islands. About 10,000 people—one-fifth of the island's population—left Jersey, and about half of Guernsey's population found places on the ships going to Britain. On Sark, the Dame, Mrs. Sibyl Hathaway, set her face against evacuation and reminded her people sharply that you do not leave home just because the enemy is at the gate; nearly everybody decided to stay. But there was panic on Alderney. At a public meeting almost everybody decided to leave after Judge French had painted a grim picture of the reality of a German Occupation. The rule would be 'two suitcases for every nose', and all cattle and other livestock had to be left behind. Only about one dozen people chose to remain on the island.

Guernsey was left to take responsibility for the confusion left behind on Alderney, and a rescue team of farmers and ambulance-men was sent to the island to remove the people who remained behind by force if necessary, and to retrieve all the cattle and pigs that they could find. What else they, or subsequent rescue teams from Guernsey both official and unofficial, retrieved is a matter of continuing argument between the islands. The leaders of the expedition insist to this day that it was properly organised and that it was performing a strictly humanitarian mission. Those left behind on Alderney, and those who later claimed to have found long-lost possessions in Guernsey houses after the war, tell a different story.

The only unbiased view, perhaps, comes from an Irishman called Peter Doyle, who was accepted by the Germans as a neutral and who lived on Alderney for ten months between 1941 and 1942. Doyle is now dead, but in a tape-recorded interview made shortly before his death he described some of the rescue operations as drunken orgies when the rescue teams found the pubs deserted but fully stocked. 'The Guernseymen did a lot of damage', he said. One Alderney publican had left behind a notice reading: 'I have left you the stocks, please respect the property'. But after liberal quantities of the stocks had been consumed, the rescue party, according to Doyle, were in no mood to do any rescuing. Instead they shot the cattle they found, and Doyle said graphically: 'The damage was terrible. There were horses and cows dead in the streets. Poultry lived on the carcasses. When the Germans landed they thought they would get the blame. They had to clean up the mess. They christened Alderney the arse of the world'.

To be fair, Doyle did stress that French fishermen were also guilty of looting on Alderney. Guernsey leaders have always

insisted that everyone on the rescue expeditions behaved correctly
and that there was no looting. When, later in the war, some
Guernseymen were caught looting on Alderney they were heavily
punished by the civil authorities on Guernsey.

The story of the Occupation years is told graphically in the
various Occupation Museums on the Channel Islands; in the
official history of the Occupation, *The German Occupation of the
Channel Islands* by Charles Cruickshank; and in the various books
of personal reminiscences of the war years which abound in
Channel Island bookshops. Inevitably, opinion varies according
to individual experiences. Alderney undoubtedly suffered most.
It was used as a slave labour camp by the Germans, and there is a
memorial to the many prisoners who died there in what were
undoubtedly horrific circumstances. But Doyle, an on-the-spot
witness, tells too of some groups of Todt workers, such as
Algerians, Moroccans and French, who were actually given one
month off in every six; and he also suggested in an interview that
the deaths among prisoners and slave workers would have been
fewer if the guards had not been using their rations as a basis for
a thriving black market in neighbouring Normandy and
Brittany.

In Jersey and Guernsey, the people suffered increasing deprivation and hardship, and things got tougher as the years went on
because the quality of the German troops sent to garrison the
islands inevitably got lower. The tricks used by the islanders to
listen to BBC news bulletins, to avoid handing over all their
produce to the Germans, or to enjoy some of the everyday goods
which had become luxuries, were manifold. In these conditions
the farmers and fishermen were obviously at an advantage, but
cooperation at all levels—with some particularly wise leadership
on Jersey and an impressive grassroots communal survival
exercise in Guernsey—meant that most people had sufficient
food and clothing. Commando raids on the islands, which
Churchill was particularly keen on during the early days of the
Occupation, were generally unsuccessful and eventually petered
out. The islanders were not sorry. The commandos could not
improve their lot; and German retribution could be harsh. The
post-war picture painted by historians of 'the brave little Channel

Islands' was exaggerated, but so too are tales of collaboration. Certainly the Channel Islanders collaborated with the Germans, but for the most part they did so because that was the only way to survive in day-to-day life. Their loyalty to Britain remained constant, despite the unseemly haste with which they had been abandoned to their fate.

And there was none more loyal than the Dame of Sark, who left the Germans in no doubt about who was in charge of her island. As a result Sark was relatively untouched by the Occupation, although its very remoteness must have meant that the five years of Occupation were long and frightening ones for the people.

Despite the exigencies of war, the Channel Islanders' capacity for wit and inventiveness did not falter. Guernseymen and Jerseymen, continuing their historic rivalry yet never carrying it too far, plotted to ensure that supplies intended for the other island should, in fact, remain where they were for local use. Straight-faced officials did their best to mystify the German authorities with figures—and often succeeded. When Guernsey's Agricultural Officer, Raymond Falla, was accused of not giving the Germans the correct total of cows on the island he suggested that they might like to count them for themselves—a project which would undoubtedly have involved the whole island in a gigantic game of hide-the-heifer. But the Germans wisely declined. The Germans got their own back at one meeting in Guernsey: they suggested that as the island's principal industry before the war was catering for holidaymakers, the inhabitants had become unused to hard work. And there was humour. The islanders will still tell you of a German soldier who remarked wisely to a Jerseyman: 'I know you are all longing to see our backsides'.

But it was 1945 before that was to happen. By then the Germans had converted the islands into a series of fortresses. Alderney's Napoleonic defences had been extensively added to, and the island resembled a huge battleship. Guernsey and Jersey had both been adorned with gigantic gun emplacements and warrens of bunkers and earthworks which served the dual purpose of commanding the Channel approaches and making the islands virtually impregnable to any attack.

As the Allies swept through Europe after D-Day in 1944, the Channel Islands became an isolated outpost. They could not be liberated because the islanders themselves would have suffered unacceptable casualties in any invasion. For a time there was a fear that the Nazis would make a last stand on the islands and that the Channel Islands, along with the Alps of Bavaria and Austria, would be the scene of the much vaunted 'final redoubt'.

But, in the event, the end came quietly. After Hitler's death his successor, Admiral Doenitz, wanted only to get the war over with, and it was the Germans on the Channel Islands rather than the islanders who feared for their lives on VE Day. Expecting retribution and bloodshed, they doubled all their guards as Churchill made his famous speech announcing the end of hostilities and adding: 'Our dear Channel Islands are also to be freed today'. British warships quickly appeared off the islands and troops stormed ashore half expecting trouble. There was none. Fears about what might have been happening on Sark, where flames had been flickering by night, proved groundless: the formidable Dame was, as usual, a jump ahead of everybody else, had built a celebration bonfire, and was already supervising the occupying German troops in the various tasks of clearing up the island to which she had allocated them.

With British financial help, the islands quickly recovered from their ordeal. But to this day visible evidence of the Occupation of Guernsey and Jersey remains, in the shape of the gun emplacements and towers at strategic points on the two islands. Ideally, the islands would like to see these removed. But the Germans did their job well: on such small islands it would be too dangerous and too costly to destroy them.

FOUR

People and Places

The more that one visits the Channel Islands, and the harder one tries to get to know them and their people, the more one realises what a complicated little community — or, rather, series of communities — they are. Their history has been shaped by the Great Power politics which have gone on around them; politics which have often seen the islands at the centre of an international tug-of-war. And their geography has been shaped by their history — their coastlines bristling with the defence installations of the last five centuries, and their interiors a jumble of zig-zagging farm tracks which, only comparatively recently, have been tarred over and turned into proper roads. The results is that on Jersey, for instance, you can drive more than 500 miles during a week's stay and still not have covered every piece of road on an island which measures only nine miles by five. Many of these roads appear to lead to nowhere in particular, especially on Guernsey, and as they are often badly sign-posted, or not sign-posted at all, it is easy to get lost. One is reminded of the lanes of Devon and Cornwall, often lying lower than the fields above them and darkened by thick hedges, where the locals will laugh at those who get lost at night and blame the 'pixies'. The only difference is that in the Channel Islands help, in the form of a farm, or the lights of traffic on a main road, is never far away.

I was introduced to this maze of roads on Guernsey by an elderly coach driver with whom I often used to have a quiet drink on summer evenings. He had been born and bred on the island, and after I had made several visits there it became his joke to announce: 'Tonight I will show you a bit of Guernsey that you have never seen before'. For many weeks he succeeded in doing just that; picking his way unerringly through lanes where the trees and hedgerows grew so thickly that we seemed to be in a tunnel, he would find his way back to the beauty spots of his own childhood: a vantage point from which one looked across peaceful farmland; one of the less frequented 'water lanes' where paths precariously follow tumbling streams down to the sea on the south coast; a deserted corner of the Common where rabbits played among the gorse in the twilight; a secret footpath which approached some well-known landmark from a completely different angle; or a hidden crevice in the cliffs from which, protected from the elements, we watched an endless sea, perhaps topped by angry white foam, crashing timelessly against the rocks far below.

My coach driver, Bill Martin, would chuckle with quiet delight when I confessed that yes, he had again shown me something entirely new. 'When you can be blindfolded, driven round the island for an hour, get out of the car, take the blindfold off, and know exactly where you are, then you will really know Guernsey' he used to say. It is a test which no visitor, and I suspect few Guernseymen, could guarantee to pass. But I like to think that, before he died, Bill Martin did show me much of the hidden face of the island.

On such exploratory excursions, on any of the islands, one is always struck by how strongly agricultural they remain. The tourism industry grows, and the settlers may move in from the mainland and the Continent with their private fortunes (as on Jersey), with their business interests (as on Guernsey), their pensions (as on Alderney), or just their dreams (as on Sark), but all the islands remain predominantly farming communities. Even on Jersey, where tourism is such a huge industry, well over half of the land area is still given over to farming; and when one also takes into account the unusable heathland, the parks, the golf courses and the gardens, it is small wonder that Jersey, like the other islands, is still so green. Indeed, one cannot imagine that this state of affairs will ever change. History has taught the islanders the advantages of self-sufficiency, but even if that were not the case there would always be farmers there because the attractions of rich soil and mild winters are too strong to ignore. It is possible to have a double crop of potatoes, and the first of these can be on the market in England long before any home-grown variety. Broccoli and lettuce have been popular post-war crops. And the farms have also found that it pays to have a foot in the flower market: daffodils, iris, anemones and gladioli are all early spring crops, while roses are increasingly popular and carnations have joined tomatoes as a very profitable crop under glass.

And then, of course, there are the world-famous Channel Island breeds of cattle: the Jersey, the Guernsey, and the Alderney. These cattle epitomise the inter-island rivalries, and although the islands' respective layouts and the tendency towards small farms both mean that one seldom sees large herds, visitors will seldom go long before seeing a solitary beast, or a group of three or four, chewing contentedly in some lush but unexpected corner. In some areas individual cows are often tethered, and in chilly weather a coat or sack is often put over the animal — a gesture which does not only demonstrate the regard in which these cattle are held, but which is also said to improve the breed. Dairy products are, of course, superb.

The island farmhouses are often very old and built of granite. Many of them are in Norman style, massively walled and, with their small windows, somehow resembling fortresses. But they have mellowed with the years, and the stonework is often richly tinted with lichens. Inside they are functional and well cared for; snugly warm and draught-free in the winter and sharing with many old English farmhouses the peculiar ability to remain warm even when an outside door is left open, and cool and shaded in the summer.

Besides the castles and other historical buildings mentioned later, the only other buildings of architectural note are the few surviving manor houses. In most cases these have been rebuilt on very old foundations so that, with the exception of St. Ouen's Manor in Jersey, they no longer resemble the châteaux in neighbouring Normandy on which they are supposed to have been modelled. One of the benefits of the influx of wealthy people into the islands, usually for tax or health reasons, is that houses like these, which might otherwise have fallen into disrepair, are greatly in demand and in many cases are lovingly repaired, restored, and maintained, and such historic features as granite arches or stone mounting blocks outside become features of the house instead of being lost in a tangle of weeds and shrubs.

As opposed to the manor houses, the churches of Jersey and Guernsey are modelled on the early English Norman churches: solid, formidable, yet surprisingly beautiful. Most have towers or spires, and an island oddity is that after they had been built some churches became too small for the increasing population and were enlarged by adding a second, twin aisle. Thus the congregation can all find seats, but their view of the chancel and pulpit may well be obscured by the thick pillars of what was once an outside wall.

The churches are still at the centre of the parishes into which the islands are divided, so that the feeling of continuity is even greater in the Channel Islands than elsewhere—and this continuity is even greater than might be immediately apparent to the eye of the visitor. Feudalism is not confined to Sark— seigneurial rights exist on all the islands, and even the Queen is entitled to some tithes although they are due to her not as Queen of England but as (in the eyes of the islanders) Duke of Normandy. Most of the tithes are still known under their original French names: *poulage* (chicken rent), *chapeau de roses* (crown of roses), and *rente du blé* (wheat tithe). But in most cases they have been converted into a cash payment, and the rights to these ancient payments are bought and sold like stocks and shares.

The islanders themselves are a very mixed people, insularity having been sharply reversed by the heavy immigration of recent years. The financial advantage which many of the immigrants had over native islanders has caused problems on Jersey and Guernsey where, for example, a young married couple who had grown up on the island could not hope to buy a house because prices had been so inflated by demand from the wealthy newcomers. As a result, housing is now divided up according to size and rateable value, and only those with long-term residential qualifications are entitled to buy the smaller, and therefore cheaper, properties. But such practical problems resulting from the rapid growth in population have not been matched by personal ones. The native-born islander—intelligent, hard-working, ambitious and quick-witted—has often been more than a match in business for his overseas competitor, and the distribution of wealth on the islands has caused few problems to date.

All the islanders are acutely conscious of the environment, as befits the inhabitants of one of the world's crowded corners, and determined that the islands shall remain attractive holiday destinations. Control over development is strict—as is police action against vandalism or such hazards as excessively noisy late-night revelry. In small communities such as these public opinion is not only important but can also make itself strongly felt. But the visitor is welcome—and the islander is helpful and hospitable. Over the years I have been invited to many of the islanders' homes, and one is quickly accepted and treated as a friend in shops, bars, or simply on the street.

The growth of tourism, which jerked the Channel Islands so roughly into the reality of the twentieth century, has not caused the surly resentment which can be found in so many parts of the world. Rather, the islanders seem determined to benefit from its advantages as much as any visitor.

The islanders are nothing if not industrious—something which, in the past, has caused problems. For Jersey was, of course, the island which gave its name to knitwear. In the Middle Ages, the impecunious islanders used to provide themselves with clothes from the wool of the then prevalent sheep, and by the sixteenth century they found that they had created a fashion and items of jersey, meaning knitted goods, were in such demand in England, and fetched such high prices, that people began to neglect the farming and fishing by which they made a living and turned to their needles in such numbers that the States of Jersey became seriously alarmed by the neglect of these essential industries and in 1608 passed a law forbidding anyone over the age of 15 from knitting during seed time, the harvest, or the seaweed-gathering season. The fashion passed, but 'jersey' and 'guernsey' sweaters, usually machine-knitted but finished by hand, are still in demand.

Because of their geographical situation, the Channel Islands contain various species of flora which are not found anywhere else in the British Isles. Due to the intense farming many plants which are unique to the islands are hard to find, but the botanist might do well to direct his steps towards the unspoiled stretches of St. Ouen's Bay on Jersey and Grand Havre on Guernsey, both of which are backed by common land. Spring visitors cannot fail to notice the wild yellow wallflowers on the walls of Mont Orgueil Castle in Jersey, while loose-flowered orchids can be found in some marshy corners of the island. The Jersey Fern emanates from North Africa, and is found in few places in Europe, while some of the mosses, lichens and fungi in which the islands are so rich are sub-alpine, particularly on the high cliffs of Guernsey's south coast.

FIVE

Jersey—St. Helier

The Normans christened Jersey. They called it 'Gersey'—or 'grassy isle'. Now the French call it *'La Reine de la Manche'*, or 'Queen of the Channel'. And between the wars British holiday-makers used to call it the 'honeymoon island' because it was so popular with newlyweds. In fact Jersey—the most southerly of the British Isles and the largest of the Channel Islands—is ideal for holidaymakers of every age. It has big, safe, sandy beaches; lively nightlife; superb shops; some of the best hotels in Europe; dramatic seascapes and cliff scenery; quiet countryside where Jersey cattle graze in rich green fields; glorious woodland walks; historic castles; good restaurants with international menus; and a wealth of interesting sightseeing trips. And all this is squeezed into a roughly rectangular island, nine miles by five, with an area of about 45 square miles. It is little wonder, therefore, that many British holidaymakers 'going abroad' for the first time choose to go to Jersey—and even though, strictly speaking, they are not abroad, the island has an exciting Continental atmosphere which, coupled with low prices, easy access and familiar customs, makes it one of Europe's most attractive holiday destinations.

The island's capital is St. Helier, which is home to about half of the island's population. Even St. Helier's greatest admirers will readily admit that it is not a pretty town. It is built around the rather ugly harbour, and is divided by the massive rock on which stands the Napoleonic Fort Regent. The narrow streets are crowded, and the introduction of pedestrian shopping precincts has necessitated having a nightmarish one-way traffic system. St.

Helier has also managed to retain a faintly Victorian air in parts — particularly along the seafront where exposure to winter gales has prevented any planting of trees to soften the effect.

But it is a town which tries hard to be liked, and its charms grow on you. Behind the seafront are some attractive little squares and gardens, and the shops — which reflect the island's general air of prosperity — are magnificent. Their window displays are a constant temptation to visitors, who linger outside comparing prices with what they would have to pay at home. Duty-free and V.A.T.-free shopping means that spirits, wine, tobacco, perfume, jewellery, watches, photographic equipment, radios, and other luxury goods are all considerably cheaper in the Channel Islands than elsewhere.

For the visitor St. Helier also has an imposing number of restaurants, dance halls, cabarets, discos, and other places of entertainment — while Fort Regent has been far-sightedly and imaginatively converted into a leisure and sports complex where one can do anything from walking in the rose gardens laid out on the old walls of the fort to eating, shopping, swimming in a national-sized indoor pool, or 'ice skating' on a rink with plastic 'ice'.

Fort Regent overlooks the Harbour, the curiously unattractive focal point of the town and the spot at which the car ferries from Britain and France arrive. The ferries will always be an important factor in the island's communications with Britain and the Continent, because sea mists sometimes close the airport for a day or two, particularly in late spring and early summer. The ferries are seldom affected by this hazard, and still pick their way carefully past Elizabeth Castle, which stands on an islet in St. Aubin's Bay, about three-quarters of a mile offshore from St. Helier.

Jersey did not have a proper harbour until 1700, and its haphazard development in the nineteenth century as traffic increased rapidly no doubt accounts for its present piecemeal appearance. Even today it loses much of its water at low tide, giving it the appearance of a large and somewhat grubby puddle. Evidently it was suffering from a similar disadvantage in 1846 when Queen Victoria visited the island, for Prince Albert — not noted for sarcasm — was moved to inquire of his hosts: 'Tell me,

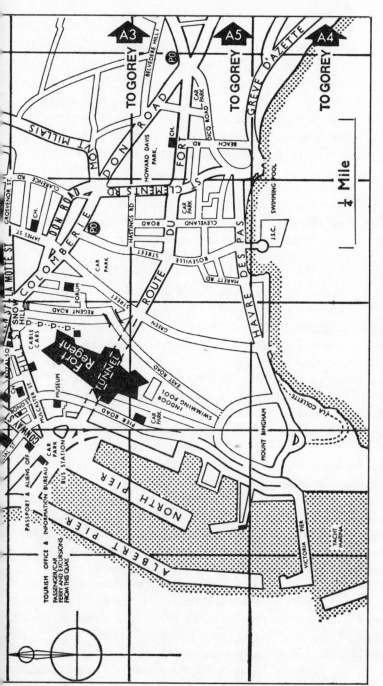

TOWN OF ST. HELIER

why do you Jerseymen always build your harbours on dry land?'
The answer to that question lies partly with the might of the
Atlantic beyond the harbour walls, for attempts to construct new
outer breakwaters have always been smashed by heavy seas.

Although it is never beautiful the Harbour is nevertheless, like
all harbours, a good place to stand and stare; the inner basin is
always full of yachts and other small boats. Above the Harbour is
the Weighbridge, a word of special significance on an island
where, after tourism, farming is still the main business. It is here
that the States operate the busy scales where crops are inspected
and graded before being shipped off the island, and in season a
stream of lorries carrying potatoes and tomatoes arrives at the
Weighbridge every morning from country districts.

As much of the Harbour dries out at low tide, one can walk
over the sands of St. Aubin's Bay towards Elizabeth Castle which,
with Fort Regent, dominates the town. Elizabeth Castle was built
between 1590 and 1600, and was named by Sir Walter Raleigh,
then Governor of the island, in honour of Queen Elizabeth I. In
the seventeenth century, when Jersey was a Royalist stronghold,
it was besieged for 50 days as local forces held out against the
expedition sent to Jersey by the Parliamentarians in 1651 to crush
Royalist resistance.

But the island on which Elizabeth Castle stands has a far longer
history than the castle itself. The adjacent Hermitage Rock was
once the home of a sixth-century hermit called Helibert, or
Helerius, who attempted to stamp out piracy in the area with
words as his only weapon. In the year 555 he was killed by a pirate
captain who feared the effects of his oratory. But the hermit's
memory lived on, and he became a cult personality. A tiny
memorial chapel was built on the rock and later, as St. Helier,
the hermit became patron saint of the island's main church.

Although it is picturesque when seen from a distance,
especially at night when it is attractively floodlit, the castle,
bought by the States of Jersey for £1,500 in 1922 and extensively
renovated and repaired, in fact consists of a number of modern
buildings. As well as the ramparts, and attractive picnic areas
within the grounds, visitors to the castle can see tableaux
depicting scenes from the castle's history. There is also a German

bunker with relics of the Second World War. During the Occupation of the island the Germans used the castle as a strong-hold. Elizabeth Castle also contains the Jersey Militia Museum, with relics dating back to the Napoleonic era, but the castle's most famous exhibit is probably 'Jersy Lily' Langtry's famous gold pistol.

The most interesting part of the castle itself is the keep. Its gateway is crowned by the arms of Queen Elizabeth I. A breakwater links the castle with Hermitage Rock. At low tide the island is connected to the rest of Jersey by a causeway, but when the causeway is under water amphibious DUKWs run a shuttle service between the castle and the shore.

Fort Regent, St. Helier's other most prominent landmark, crowns a rocky promontory which rises abruptly in the centre of the town just east of the harbour. The rock is known as Le Mont de la Ville, or Town Hill, and has long been a military strongpoint. In 1550, St. Helier's leaders received a Royal instruction that, in case of foreign invasion, 'because ... you have no place of strength to retire unto, we require you to convey your Town unto the hill above the same, which we be informed may with little charge be made strong and defensible'. Fortifications were built there during the sixteenth century, when Spain was posing a military threat to Britain, and during the eighteenth century when the enemy was France. The present fortifications, which include a 233-feet-deep well, cover four acres and were built between 1806 and 1814 when there were fears for Jersey's safety during the Napoleonic Wars. In fact Fort Regent—named after the Prince Regent, later King George IV—never saw action and after the Second World War (during which German troops were housed there) the buildings were seen as something of a white elephant.

In recent years, however, a road tunnel has pierced the hill and the fort has come to life again as a £4 million development plan has turned it into an entertainment complex. The 22-acre site, which can be reached by cable car from Snow Hill, has given the developers plenty of scope. Besides the swimming pool, sports halls, and the more obvious children's and fairground-style en-tertainments, there are beautiful gardens including a water garden, a walk-through aviary, and an indoor piazza which is ideal for a rainy evening and which includes such attractions as an aquarium, a doll's museum, an art gallery, and a postal museum.

Above Fort Regent stand a series of flagstaffs, overlooking St. Helier Harbour. For the initiated, or for those purchasing *The Jersey Tide Tables, Fishing and Marine Guide,* the various combinations of flags and pennants raised provide a great deal of information about what is happening, or about to happen, in the harbour — from the impending arrival of a mailboat to the rather more rarely signalled occurence: 'Foreign Man-o'-War Steering for the Island'.

St. Helier's attractive shopping centre, hidden in the side streets behind the rather sombre seafront, is centred on the pedestrian precincts of King Street and Queen Street, and on Colomberie, Bath Street, The Parade and Halkett Place. Because of the low price of luxury goods, which predominate in the windows, many of the shops stay open late on summer evenings and the official early closing day, Thursday, is often ignored.

But visitors might spend their time almost as profitably exploring the older town streets, many of them still bearing their picturesque French names. The change to English names for many of the main streets has not always been an improvement: Church Street, once bisected by a small brook or gutter full of running water, used to be called Rue Trousse Cotillon, which means Tuck-up-Your-Petticoat street; and the old name for Regent Road was Rue du Froid Vent (Cold Wind Street). Colomberie took its name from the colombier, or dovecoat, which formerly stood beside the road, and the hills leading down into the town still bear French names: Mont à l'Abbé, Mont au Prêtre, Mont Cochon and Mont Millais.

At the centre of St. Helier are Royal Square and the Parish Church. The church, the oldest building in St. Helier, dates from the tenth century in parts, and was restored between 1864 and 1886. It has a square tower, which is unusual in Jersey, and some good stained glass.

Royal Square was originally the market place, and has at its centre a gilded statue of George II — although he may not be immediately recognisable as he is wearing the costume of a Roman emperor complete with laurel wreath on his head. The statue was erected in 1751 by a local hotelier, who was responsible for changing the plan to put a giant sundial on the spot after some clearance work in the square. Local wits were not impressed by the change of plan, and suggested that the statue was not of the King at all, but was simply one which the hotelier had been able to buy cheaply from a privateer. Their suggestion can be discounted, for the King wears at his knee a decoration which no Roman emperor ever saw: the Order of the Garter.

The statue is the official centre of St. Helier, and the spot from which all the island's mileages are reckoned. This is as it should be, for Royal Square has always been at the centre of island activities: as market place, meeting place, and place of execution and punishment (Jersey, in less somnambulant days, had a stern penal code: convicted witches were publicly strangled and burnt, unmarried mothers were flogged, the pillory was in use for forgery as late as 1835, and in 1619 one forerunner of today's holidaymakers, Katherine Le Sauteur, was put in the stocks for a day for the crime of 'joining in night revels dressed as a man'). Royal Square was also the scene of the melodramatic Battle of Jersey in 1781, when the Jersey Militia disobeyed a 'surrender order' to rout a French invasion force.

On the south side of the square are the States Chambers or Houses of Parliament, the Royal Court House, and the public library. The States Chambers is in Jacobean style and opened in 1887. It is the meeting place for the government, or the Assembly of the States, which is composed of 12 Senators, Jersey's elder statesmen; 12 Constables, each head of a parish; and 29 Deputies, 10 of whom represent St. Helier. All States members are unpaid. They are presided over by the Bailiff, and visitors will note that he sits higher than the Lieutenant Governor although the latter is the Queen's representative. The Lieutenant Governor, the Dean, the Attorney General and the Solicitor General, who are all appointed by the Crown, also sit in the States and are entitled to speak but not to vote. The banner above the Bailiff's seat, with three heraldic leopards on it, is also the arms of the Queen — but the Bailiff has permission to use this as his official seal.

The Royal Court House, which is open to the public, is one of the most historic buildings in Jersey. The present edifice is the

90-year-old successor to the previous Court House which dated back to the twelfth century. There are a number of interesting pictures in the hall, including a Gainsborough. Sittings of the Court are open to the public, and although French is the official language of the Court, hearings are usually conducted in English. The Court consists of 12 Jurats or magistrates, and is presided over by the Bailiff. Much of Jersey's legal and political system dates from the Norman period, notably Le Grand Coutumier which is the basis of Common Law in Jersey. There is a prisoners' cage in a corner of the Court, once necessary because there are no police cells in the Royal Court building. The silver and gilt mace which rests before the President of the Court was presented to the island, which had been the first place to recognise him as King, by Charles II ' as a proof of his royal affection towards the Island of Jersey in which he had been twice received in safety when excluded from the remainder of his dominions'.

The library, founded in 1736 by Philip Falle, Jersey's first historian, now has more than 90,000 books.

The serious nature of the work done in these three buildings, and the disturbance caused when Royal Square was used as a market, gave rise to the market being moved. Today the Markets are in Halkett Place and Beresford Street, and include daily meat and vegetable markets in a new set of informal buildings attractively set out around a central ornamental fountain and fish pond, decorated with ferns. It is here that visitors are most likely to hear the ancient Norman-French patois being spoken.

Also worth visiting is the Jersey Museum and the Barreau Art Gallery at 9 Pier Road, a merchant's house dating from 1815. The Museum is run by the Société Jersiaise, and contains the island's principal historic treasures, among them relics of Neanderthal man as well as items of bronze, silver and gold. The historical items include the Proclamation of Charles II as King nailed to the Court door in Jersey when news arrived of his father's execution — document which was to earn the island the Parliamentarians' ire and a King's gratitude. Period rooms such as the 'Jersey Bedroom' and the 'Jersey Kitchen' have been carefully reconstructed, using furniture and materials gleaned from old houses on the island. Also among the exhibits is 'Jersey Lily'

Langtry's ornate travelling case. A marine exhibit demonstrates the extent of Jersey's offshore life — ranging from the octopus and the electric ray to the mother-of-pearl-shelled ormer. The Art Gallery contains a collection of paintings by local artists, including eighteenth-century and nineteenth-century landscapes.

Above the town, look out for the Victorian Gothic edifice of Victoria College, the island's public school for boys and built between 1850 and 1852. It was named after the Queen, who took a personal interest in the school and presented to it the Winterhalter portraits of herself and Prince Albert which hang in the Assembly Hall.

St. Helier has many places of entertainment, some cheap and some pricey. But the town's biggest and best entertainment — the annual Battle of Flowers — costs nothing at all. This famous and extremely colourful annual carnival is always held on the second Thursday in August, and is very popular with locals and visitors alike. Nowadays, the word 'Battle' is a misnomer. After the parade of dozens of floats, lavishly decorated with flowers, along the seafront in Victoria Avenue, competitors and onlookers used to pull the floats to pieces and pelt one another with the blossoms. But the crowds which gather to watch are now so large that this is impossible, and the Battle has a peaceful if spectacular conclusion.

It is still a picturesque event, however, complete with bands, drum majorettes, carnival figures, and a beauty queen. There is keen competition among commercial firms and individuals on Jersey every year as to who will produce the best float. These are constructed on movable vehicles such as lorries, tractors, and even bicycles, and one float may contain tens of thousands of blossoms gathered by the entrants and their supporters. Sadly the blossoms do not last long, but the Battle of Flowers is a unique and memorable event in which everybody, but especially photographers, will delight.

Jersey's best hotels are mostly situated outside St. Helier, often in prime positions beside one or other of the better known beaches. But what I believe to be the best hotel in the Channel Islands is situated just outside St. Helier, and consists of an historic old manor house which has been brought very much up-to-date. This is the Longueville Manor Hotel, which is extremely comfortable despite the fact that the buildings date back to the sixteenth century in parts and the manor itself can be traced back as far as 1367. A former owner of the property, the Rev. W. B. Bateman, recorded in his diary more than 100 years ago that the manor was 'a wretched tumble-down old place, unfit for any decent people to live in'. But he started the work of rebuilding and restoration which has been completed by the present owners, Mr. and Mrs. Neal Lewis. The transformation has been dramatic. The hotel, standing in 15 acres of garden, meadowland and woods, is an imposing, ivy-clad house one and a half miles east of St. Helier, and three-quarters of a mile from the sea. It has its own riding stables and heated outdoor swimming pool, deliberately limits itself to 36 bedrooms (all with private bathroom or shower), has a fine oak-panelled dining-room in which excellent meals are served, and — under careful supervision and management — it sets a high standard of service. The Longueville Manor Hotel fully deserves its four-star (or, on Jersey, four-'sun') rating — the highest attainable on the island.

Other hotels in town include the Beaufort and the Pomme d'Or, both of which seem better suited to business traffic than to catering for holidaymakers; the centrally situated and modern Apollo; the friendly Alexandra; and the Chelsea which is a good family hotel. The Mayfair is cheap and cheerful, and fun in the winter. With new building almost impossible, a number of old-established hotels have recently undergone facelifts.

Boarding houses, which now prefer to be called private hotels, are reasonably priced and often set surprisingly high standards. Many of them have built cocktail bars and even swimming pools for their guests, and the pre-war image of fearsome landladies has gone for ever. A young couple holidaying on the island told me that they feared the worst when their landlady asked what time they would be back that evening. They replied that they thought it would be about midnight and, afraid that they might be locked out, hesitantly asked why. 'Oh', replied the landlady, 'I just wanted to make sure that you would be back in time for our little party in the bar — but it never gets going until about midnight so you'll be all right'.

SIX

Exploring Jersey

There is a baby called Bamenda who is under the firm impression that I am her father. She gazes trustingly into my eyes, makes cooing noises, and holds firmly on to my finger with her own tiny fist. Occasionally, when she is feeling playful, she chuckles and tries to take off my glasses.

And I would not mind if it were not for the fact that her real father, who lives on Jersey, has a chest measurement roughly twice mine, bends iron bars with his bare hands, is exceptionally hairy, and tends to display extreme jealousy and bad temper both in public and in private.

Bamenda's father is Jambo, a massive lowland gorilla who has the distinction of being the first male gorilla to be born in captivity as well as being the first to be reared successfully by his mother. And he is one of the more exotic inhabitants of author and naturalist Gerald Durrell's zoo in Jersey.

Jersey Zoo is not dedicated to the display of animals or to public entertainment, but to the preservation and breeding of some of the world's rarer species. And that, in itself, can be fascinating—as any visitor to the Zoo will agree after spending a summer afternoon watching a group of baby gorillas (including Bamenda, and for all the world like human babies) playing on the lawn outside the Zoo's main building.

The Zoo is in the 20-acre grounds of the fifteenth-century Les Augres Manor, Trinity, in the north of the island. It was set up by Gerald Durrell, and today it is the headquarters of the Jersey Wildlife Preservation Trust, an international organisation dedicated to the preservation of threatened species of mammals, birds and reptiles all over the world. You will not find any elephants, rhinoceros, giraffes or zebras in Jersey Zoo — Jersey is not the place for them, and they are not threatened species anyway. What you will find are families of lowland gorillas and Sumatran orang-utans, lots of lively but very rare lemurs, and colonies of birds threatened with imminent extinction. In the words of Gerald Durrell, Director of the Jersey Wildlife Preservation Trust: 'In the past, most zoos have been accused of being consumers rather than producers of wildlife, and to a large extent this has been true since breeding efforts in many zoos were small or non-existent. Now, however, it is essential for any zoological collection not only to breed the animals it keeps, but to be able to breed sufficient so that they may go to other collections throughout the world. We are rather proud of our export figures.'

Whenever I return to Jersey, the Zoo is one of the first places that I make for. Its lovely grounds and relaxed atmosphere are a tonic at any time of the year, but, more than anything else, Jersey Zoo is a place where visitors quickly feel *involved*. This involvement is heightened by the informative plaques attached to many of the cages, saying where its occupants come from, why they are a threatened species, and what is being done to save them. The Zoo's successes are proudly recorded, too — such as the case of the rare white-eared pheasant from north-west China and Tibet, of which there were just 18 individuals in world zoos in 1969. Between 1969 and 1975, no fewer than 112 of these birds were reared at Jersey Zoo, and they have been sent to zoos in 12 other countries. The white-eared pheasant is safe for the present.

A similar problem has arisen with the bare-faced ibis, a bird whose last three breeding grounds could shortly be wiped out by the advance of civilisation. A man-made breeding ground, carefully constructed so that the birds will not fight over nesting sites, has been built at the Zoo — and the small flock of birds have now started hatching eggs.

Local people obviously feel even more involved than the visitors. The Zoo has been especially successful at breeding lowland gorillas and when one of their female gorillas was having a baby not long ago, and had to be watched around the clock on closed-circuit television to make sure that nothing went wrong, the Zoo appealed for volunteers to spend a few hours each keeping watch. Among those who came forward were an immigrant millionairess, a foreign waiter from one of the hotels, and a retired British Rail train driver.

The baby gorillas are looked after in a nursery at Les Augres Manor — a room equipped with cots, baby baths, playpens, lots of nappies and baby bottles, and even a picture of Donald Duck painted on the ceiling. The latter is not there to amuse the keepers, however — it is a practical aid in getting the babies to focus their eyes. For the first two years of their life the gorillas bear a remarkable similarity to human babies, playing the same mischievous tricks but having the same need for care and affection. Visitors to the Zoo cannot see this nursery, but they can see the babies at play outside nearly every day. Among them is Bamenda, sired by the moody Jambo who is as popular with the crowds as are his offspring. Jambo mostly enjoys the attention — but sometimes he demonstrates his massive strength in a frightening display of ill-temper.

The Sumatran orang-utans have also bred successfully at the Zoo, with Gina, the mother of two babies, often to be seen swinging athletically around her cage with a baby clinging desperately to her fur. Such exhibitions are quite safe, for Gina is an excellent mother. Goeldi's monkeys are another species which have bred successfully in Jersey, the first recorded breeding of this endangered mammal in the British Isles. A breeding programme has been set up for Edwards's pheasants, and successful attempts have been made to breed the difficult Jamaican hutias. Special efforts are also being made with marmosets and tamarins, diminutive monkeys from South and Central America threatened by the continued destruction of their environment and by their popularity for use in medical research.

The spectacled bear, lively parrots, colourful flamingoes — besides the rarer birds and mammals mentioned above one can find these favourities, too, at Jersey Zoo. But above all it is a place of information — a place in which to spend long hours and learn a little more about the threat to some of the world's loveliest creatures and the ways in which we can help.

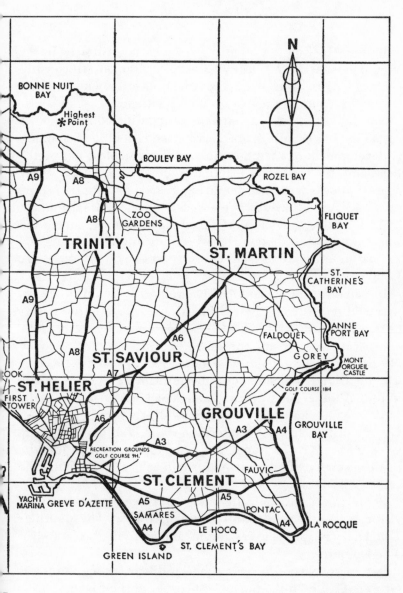

N

BONNE NUIT
BAY

* Highest
Point

BOULEY BAY

ROZEL BAY

A9   A8

A8   ZOO
GARDENS

FLIQUET
BAY

TRINITY

ST. MARTIN

ST.
CATHERINE'S
BAY

A9

ANNE
PORT BAY

FALDOUET

A8   A6

ST. SAVIOUR

GOREY

MONT
ORGUEIL
CASTLE

OOK   A7

ST. HELIER

GOLF COURSE 18H

FIRST
TOWER

GROUVILLE

A6

A3   A4

GROUVILLE
BAY

A3

RECREATION GROUNDS
GOLF COURSE 9H.

FAUVIC

ST. CLEMENT

YACHT
MARINA   GREVE D'AZETTE

A5   A5

A4

PONTAC

A4   LA ROCQUE

SAMARES

LE HOCQ

GREEN ISLAND

ST. CLEMENT'S BAY

7

| 1½ Mile |

Besides the Zoo the other place which no visitor to Jersey should miss is Mont Orgueil Castle, a dramatic thirteenth-century fortress overlooking the village of Gorey, with its pretty fishing harbour, on the east coast of the island.

Not that one is likely to miss the castle, which dominates the coast line. It is beautifully preserved, and is floodlit in summer. A development of a tenth-century military strongpoint on the headland, the castle was originally intended to guard Jersey against attacks from neighbouring France—a country whose coastline. It is beautifully preserved, and is floodlit in summer. This defensive role was performed magnificently during the thirteenth to fifteenth centuries, when the castle was instrumental in beating off many attacks and was captured only once (see Chapter 2).

Its gateways, towers and massive walls bear witness to its impregnability. At its highest point, Mont Orgueil Castle towers 310 feet above the sea and from the water it is totally inaccessible. Of special interest are the outer entrances commanded by Harliston's Tower and the inner gateway known as Queen's Gate, where a plaque commemorates Queen Victoria's visit to the castle in 1846. Another gateway cuts through St. George's Tower to the Middle Ward and the restored twelfth-century crypt of St. George's Chapel. Also of interest are the Well, the Keep, the Crypt of St. Mary's Chapel, and Somerset Tower. Inside the castle, a small exhibition contains four tableaux depicting the castle's history.

Below the castle, the little village of Gorey is popular with visiting yachtsmen and is also a good place to eat. The Moorings Hotel has a magnificent restaurant, and you will also eat well at The Dolphin.

For many years Jersey's other military strongpoint was Grosnez Castle, in the north-west corner of the island. This is believed to have dated from the same period as Mont Orgueil Castle, but it was destroyed by the French during a period of occupation in the mid-fifteenth century and today only one of the original arches and a few crumbling walls are still standing. The ruins can be visited at any time, and often form the beginning, or the conclusion, of a cliff walk along the north coast. The cliff path between Grosnez and Plemont Point is particularly attractive.

The north coast of the island is broken up by several small, attractive and sheltered beaches which are easily accessible, plus a number of others which can be reached only by scrambling around the cliffs and where it is important to take care not to get cut off by the tide. The accessible beaches include Plemont, Grève de Lecq, Bonne Nuit Bay, Giffard Bay, Bouley Bay, Rozel Bay, and Fliquet Bay. All are safe for bathing but only the beaches of Plemont, Grève de Lecq and Rozel are all sand. Bouley is the most popular, and is reached by a twisting road used by motor clubs for hill climb events. It is a centre for sub-aqua activities. Rozel has a pretty village around it, where many people like to stop for lunch or tea.

The huge St. Catherine's breakwater divides — roughly speaking — the north coast from the east coast of the island. This east coast is dominated by Mont Orgueil Castle, but between the castle and St. Catherine's breakwater are the small beaches of St. Catherine's Bay, Archirondel, and Anne Port. All are sandy, although Anne Port has some shingle too, and all are safe for non-swimmers. The conspicuous rock by Anne Port is known as Jeffrey's Leap, a spot where criminals were once forced to leap to their deaths and where 'Jeffrey', a condemned criminal, is said to have survived the leap and thus proved his innocence but then died showing enthusiasts just how he did it.

Close to Gorey village is one of the most popular excursion spots on Jersey after the castles and the zoo: the Jersey Pottery. Here visitors can watch craftsmen making the island's now distinctive pottery — and can see the clay being thrown, cast, fettled, decorated, and finally fired in the kilns. The pottery is an attractive spot despite its commercial overtones (there is no entry charge, but the showrooms *do* beckon); there are large gardens decorated with pools and fountains, as well as a restaurant. The crafty will take a picnic.

The remainder of the east coast is taken up by the expanse of Grouville Bay — or, to give it its grander title, the Royal Bay of Grouville. Queen Victoria ordered the addition of the prefix 'Royal' after seeing the bay in 1859, and although visitors do not

always share her taste and instead make for the more popular
beaches on the south coast, the long sandy stretch of
Grouville—rocky in the south but safe for non-swimmers and
backed by sand dunes and by the links of the Royal Jersey Golf
Club—is something of a personal favourite. Pistol duels were
once staged on this beach, but today it seldom sees anything more
exciting than locals walking their dogs. The part known as Green
Island, where the inland and coast roads from St. Helier to Gorey
converge, is best for families.

Behind this stretch of coastline lie the two Neolithic tombs
mentioned in Chapter 2, the Faldouet Dolmen and La Hougue
Bie. The Faldouet Dolmen is about half a mile from Jeffrey's
Leap, and is a typical passage grave: 46-feet-long with a chamber
18-feet-wide and roofed by a 24-ton capstone. It stands in a quiet
field, about a mile from the far more popular La Hougue Bie
which is something of a major tourist attraction.

La Hougue Bie, in Grouville, has a 33-feet-long tunnel entrance
along which visitors can walk—or rather creep, as it is only 4
feet 6 inches high. The cool, dry tomb, where the temperature
remains constant whatever the weather outside, has been carefully restored after a landslide and its huge capstones are still in
place. Dramatically, it is covered by a 40-feet-high mound of
earth and rubble which can be ascended by a spiral path, and this
mound looks even higher because it is surmounted by the twin
medieval chapels of Notre Dame de la Carte and the Jerusalem
Chapel. The chapels share a single roof and look like one
building, but in fact the former was built in the twelfth century
while the Jerusalem Chapel dates from the early sixteenth
century.

A romantic legend surrounds the naming of La Hougue Bie.
A dragon is said to have lived on a marsh in Jersey, from which it
occasionally emerged to terrorise the islanders. In the best
Georgian tradition a French knight, the Lord of Hambye, crossed
to Jersey and cut off the dragon's head. But his servant murdered
the Lord of Hambye, buried his body, then returned to Hambye,
in Normandy, and told the Lady of Hambye that the dragon had
killed his master but that he in turn had killed the dragon. It was
his master's last wish, he added, that she should marry him.

The Lady of Hambye agreed, but after their marriage the new Lord of Hambye cried out aloud in his sleep that he had killed his master. The Lady of Hambye had the servant brought to trial and his crime was unmasked. The Lady then had a vast burial ground raised on the ground where the Lord of Hambye had been buried, and this became known as 'La Hougue Hambye'.

Although this story might help to explain the name of the site, this is a case where truth is stranger than fiction, for La Hougue Bie has had a romantic history. The two chapels on the mounds were subjected to an extraordinary piece of development in the eighteenth century when the owner of the site, James d'Auvergne, built a brick tower, 'La Tour d'Auvergne' or the 'Prince's Tower', over the chapels. A later owner built an hotel on the site, and also established a bowling alley, but in 1919 the site was purchased by the Société Jersiaise and in 1924 the tower was found to be unsafe and was demolished. In the same year the passage tomb was excavated.

During the Second World War the Germans used the grounds of La Hougue Bie as a military strongpoint, and there is now an Occupation Museum in an original German dug-out. There is also an interesting agricultural museum in the grounds, with a good display of old farming implements and equipment.

An interesting railway exhibit provides a memento of one of Jersey's two former railways, both now closed down and largely demolished. This is a Jersey Eastern Railway guard's van containing many interesting pictures and other exhibits. Jersey's railway age began in 1870 and the eastern line, which ran from St. Helier to Gorey and provided a link with Carteret on the French coast, was run in a very friendly and casual manner: if you missed your train the driver would often stop and reverse to pick you up. In the railway's latter years the general manager was Gilbert More, the father of stage and film star, Kenneth More. The Jersey Eastern Railway closed in 1929 and Jersey's other railway, which served St. Aubin's Bay and the west coast, lasted only another seven years.

Apart from this exhibition, the only remains of the railways today are a popular public walk along the route of the railway track in the west of the island and a few stations—one of them now used as a café and others converted into houses.

To the south-west of St. Helier are two more big, sandy beaches, St. Clement's Bay and Grève d'Azette—the latter being within easy walking distance of St. Helier. Practically in town are the two small sandy beaches of Havre des Pas.

The other side of town, of course, is the huge bay which St. Helier looks upon as its 'local' beach: the three miles of wide, sandy, south-facing beach known as St. Aubin's Bay. This bay stretches in a deep crescent from St. Helier round to the fishing village of St. Aubin, a small attractive and prosperous looking place backed by steep hills. Just off the coast at this point is another island fort, St. Aubin's Fort, which may be reached on foot at low tide. The fort dates from 1542, and its main feature is the original tower around which the outer defence works were built later. A pier was built there in the latter half of the seventeenth century, a factor which led to a brief reign by St. Aubin as the island's principal port because shipowners, merchants and ship's captains were attracted there. Later St. Helier regained its pre-eminence, and St. Aubin reverted to being a quiet fishing village, although it is officially Jersey's second town. The fort, which is in good repair, is now used for youth activities.

The road from St. Aubin climbs steeply above the town to cross the headland containing Noirmont Point and Point le Fret. Hidden between these headlands is Portelet Bay, a small 'suntrap' bay sheltered from all but southerly breezes and set in picturesque surroundings with a fine stretch of soft sand. It is overlooked by a very good holiday village, which has recently been extended and modernised and has excellent accommodation. The village does not intrude into its surroundings, and the bay is popular with the locals at weekends.

Beyond Point le Fret is St. Brelade's Bay, perhaps the best known on the island. It has a very good and lively beach, facing south, with miles of glorious sand and lots of refreshment and recreational facilities. You can water-ski there, there are beach craft for hire, and beach guards are on duty in the high season. One danger spot: the rocks to the left of the bay, which can be hazardous when the tide reaches this point. The tide, in fact, divides St. Brelade's into two bays, the second being known as Ouaisne Bay (pronounced 'weigh knee'). Also on this stretch of coast is Beau Port, a small secluded bay with a good beach backed by bracken and pinewoods. You get there on foot from St. Brelade's Bay, and it is a fine picnic spot.

To the west of St. Brelade's Bay is Corbière Point, with its picturesque lighthouse. Here the Five Mile Road sweeps down to St. Ouen's (pronounced St. Wan's) Bay, a huge four-mile stretch of sand, backed by sand dunes, which makes up most of Jersey's west coast and is the largest beach in the Channel Islands. Because of its size St. Ouen's Bay can never be crowded, and although it is rather exposed it is a popular picnic spot and is good for both swimming and surfing, although there is a strong undertow and it is wise to heed the advice of the beach guards who are on duty in the summer. In winter, especially during a westerly gale, the heavy seas can be spectacular and, as the great grey waves rise threateningly over the low lying land behind, even frightening.

Many of the island's best hotels back on to these south and west coast beaches, among them the top-graded Atlantic, St. Brelade's Bay, and Water's Edge. Also recommended is the Mermaid Hotel close to Jersey Airport which is at St. Peter, behind St. Ouen's Bay. Primarily a business and conference hotel, the Mermaid is efficiently run and its lakeside setting is pleasant for a holiday. In the restaurant bar you can find the reason for the hotel's name: a glass case on a wall containing a figure that is half human and half fish. The locals will assure you that this grisly relic was caught locally; and although the superstitious may believe it, the cynical might find their time well spent looking for stitch marks.

Jersey also caters especially for handicapped visitors at the Maison de Landes Hotel, St. Ouen. A guide for the disabled, 'Access in Jersey', is available free from the States Tourism Department at Weighbridge, St. Helier.

There are some interesting excursion spots near St. Ouen's Bay, among them the Battle of Flowers Museum, L'Etacq Woodcraft, St. Peter's Bunker, and the Jersey Motor Museum.

Jersey's annual Battle of Flowers is, by its very nature, an ephemeral event, for the flowers quickly die and one is left only with memories, and perhaps photographs, of the flower-decorated floats. The Battle of Flowers Museum at La Robeline, St. Ouen, however, contains the few floats which do last — made with dried grasses and wild flowers. The specialist in these classes is a farmer's daughter, Miss Florence Bechelet, a frequent prize winner at the Battle of Flowers, some of whose star exhibits are on permanent display here. Look out for '101 Dalmations' (there really are 101), and the wildlife scenes. Miss Bechelet, sadly no longer an annual exhibitor at the Battle of Flowers, is often in attendance and can tell you how many hours' work there is in each exhibit.

At the northern end of St. Ouen's Bay are the workshops of L'Etacq Woodcraft, where local craftsmen carve many quaint little figurines, statuettes and other novelties which can be purchased as souvenirs. A personal favourite: walking sticks made from the stalk of the giant Jersey cabbage.

St. Peter's Bunker, opposite St. Peter's Church, is one of the most popular excursions on the island where interest in the German Occupation is strong. It is a seven-roomed Second World War German bunker which now contains a huge collection of Occupation relics gathered by owner and enthusiast Richard Mayne. The Jersey Motor Museum, near St. Peter's Church, contains a display of motor vehicles dating back to the early 1900s as well as photographic mementoes of Jersey's railways and a children's corner.

One of the quieter, not to say odder, spots is the Fantastic Gardens at St. Mary's, in St. Peter's Valley. Although the gardens are attractive in their own right, and are a popular picnic spot, they provide a glimpse of the cultures and myths of other civilisations, including India, Islam, China and Japan. As well as replicas of shrines and other architectural structures from these places, the gardens contain plants and trees which have served mankind in these and other parts of the world as medicines, balms, materials for fabrics, or dyes. Plaques explain the meanings of the various structures and the uses to which the plants have been put.

Jersey's magnificent manor houses include Rozel Manor, dating from 1770 and with a medieval chapel in its grounds; St. Ouen's Manor, dating from about 1480 and restored in 1856, with its fine oak-panelled hall, staircase, and gallery; and Trinity Manor, partly Tudor, partly rebuilt in the first half of the seventeenth century, and completely restored between 1911 and 1914. None of the properties are open to the public except on special occasions, but if the opportunity does arise they are well worth visiting.

A number of the nurseries on Jersey, which produce the island's famous tomatoes, carnations, and pot plants, are open to the public, among them Haute Tombette Flower Farm, St. Mary, and the Sunset Nurseries, St. Ouen. Recommended: the Carnation Nurseries at Retreat Farm, St. Lawrence, where you can tour the glasshouses free of charge and where flowers can be despatched to order. There are refreshment facilities. The Strawberry Farm, Petit Alva, in St. Peter's Valley, is a cheap-and-cheerful-looking conglomeration of jewellery workshops, craft centre, tea rooms, and strawberry fields which contain an extraordinary exhibition of lovingly constructed stone models of many of Jersey's leading landmarks and historical buildings. You can also visit a German Occupation Bunker before enjoying a bowl of freshly picked strawberries and Jersey cream. Good car-parking facilities and the absence of an entrance fee make this a fine family outing.

Many of the parish churches in Jersey are worth a visit. St. Brelade's occupies the best site of any church on the island, nestling at the western end of St. Brelade's Bay. St. Clement's has two wall paintings, and St. Lawrence's, which has a fine Norman tower, has ancient tombstones built into the exterior of its outside walls. St. Peter's spire is the tallest in the island, and its top is lit as a warning to aircraft using the adjacent airport.

Actress Lillie Langtry, the constant companion of King Edward VII when he was Prince of Wales, is buried in St. Saviour's church-yard where a marble bust of her marks her grave.

But there are two churches of very particular interest. The first is St. Matthew's Church, Millbrook, near St. Helier, which is also known as 'the Glass Church' because it is decorated with a famous collection of Lalique glass. This dates from 1934 when a local resident, Florence Lady Trent, decided to renew the interior of the then rather plain church as a memorial to her late husband, Lord Trent. Réné Lalique, the Parisian glass worker, was invited to collaborate with an architect in the design of the windows and doors as well as the interior decorations. The glass includes a huge cross behind the altar and a striking group of angels in the Lady Chapel which are illuminated at all services. In the patterns of the glasswork can be found both the Jersey lily and the Madonna lily. The church is lit by massive Lalique glass troughs on the ceiling, and the glass font is thought to be unique. Visitors are welcome at Sunday services (11 a.m. or 7 p.m.) or community hymn singing at 8.15 p.m., and there is also community hymn singing at 8.15 on Wednesday evenings in summer when the church is lit and at its most impressive.

And finally there is the Fishermen's Chapel, next to St. Brelade's Parish Church, which is my own favourite building in the Channel Islands. It is thought to date from the middle of the sixth century in parts, and is an ancient monastic chapel used by fishermen to pray before they set sail. Also known as the 'Chapelle-les-Pêcheurs', the chapel had its walls covered with mural paintings, probably during the fourteenth century, and these were discovered in 1918 when, after a severe storm, colours appeared in the ceiling and paintings were found underneath the plaster. There is one picture of the Annunciation on the ceiling and another on the south wall together with one of the Blessed Virgin. Also on the south wall are pictures of the Magi, and a picture of a soldier wearing chain-mail. On the west wall there are pictures of the Resurrection and the Last Judgment; on the north wall King Herod and the Scourging of Christ. The north ceiling has a picture of Jesus on a donkey and a Roman soldier, and on the south ceiling there are pictures of Adam and Eve. These are best seen in damp weather. In certain atmospheric conditions which occur only once in every 50 years or so, other pictures appear.

One of the delights of Jersey is that as far as eating out and evening entertainment is concerned, the island caters for all tastes. Equally true, although perhaps less obvious, is that it caters for all pockets too. There are plenty of cheap restaurants in the island, and this is particularly true at lunchtime. You can buy sandwiches or a snack at one of the many beach kiosks, or you may prefer to go for a pub lunch—one of the highlights of the island. Although Jersey's pubs are similar to those in mainland Britain in most respects (but the local draught beers carry an unexpected kick, so take care), many of them take a special pride in their lunches, which may be anything from the traditional 'ploughman's lunch' to fairly extensive cold tables or 'pick-a-boards', where you pay a set price and eat as much as you like. These meals represent really good value in both town and country. Many pubs also serve coffee.

Jersey's cuisine is interesting for its combination of local dishes, straightforward English food, and the distinctive Continental touch brought to the island by many French and other European hoteliers, restaurateurs and chefs.

The local specialities, of course, are lobster and other sea foods, vegetables (especially salads), and dairy products. The island is so rich in sea food resources that at one time oysters and mussels used to be given away in Gorey. That, alas, is no longer the case, but the island does still have its own oyster and mussel beds, and lovers of seafoods will feel very much at home.

SEVEN

Guernsey — St. Peter Port

Guernsey is the second largest of the Channel Islands, and lies more or less at the centre of the archipelago, 30 miles off the coast of France and 80 miles from the south coast of England. It has an area of about 24 square miles, mostly agricultural land, and a population of 53,000 including more than 36,000 Guernsey born. With Alderney, Sark, Herm and Jethou it comprises the Bailiwick of Guernsey — a fact which means that the smaller islands all acknowledge the Bailiff of Guernsey as their civil head and chief of justice. But the smaller islands are still independent of Guernsey in varying degrees.

Roughly triangular in shape, with the south coast made up of cliffs, the island becomes flatter as you travel north either up the west coast — which has many fine, unspoiled, but rather exposed beaches — or up the east coast which consists largely of the towns of St. Peter Port and St. Sampson. Guernsey is much quieter than its southerly neighbour, Jersey, and the interior of the island is a maze of narrow country lanes in which the visitor can quickly get lost. Besides farmland, much of the island is given over to the raising of produce under glass: the island's tomatoes are famous. The 'Guernsey Tom' began to appear about a century ago under the name of 'love apple'. Today the tomatoes are grown in glasshouses previously used for grapes, which is why a tomato nursery is known on the island as a vinery. Some of the glasshouses are as large as aircraft hangars, containing up to 10,000 plants. Besides tomatoes, the island specialises in growing carnations, early spring flowers, gladioli, and roses. Like the

St Ouen's Bay, Jersey, with La Corbière lighthouse in the background

2 *opposite:* Guernsey's south coast, looking westwards at Les Tielles

3 *above left:* 'La Grandmère de Chimquière', Guernsey. This prehistoric stone figure representing the Earth Mother, forms one of the gateposts of the churchyard at St Martin's, and locals always say 'Good morning' to her

4 *above right:* Statue menhir in Castel churchyard, Guernsey

5 *below:* The Faldouet Dolmen, Jersey

6   A detail from *The Death of Major Peirson* by Copley. *(By courtesy of The Tate Gallery)*

7 *above:* German Prisoners of War, 1945, awaiting embarkation on transports, on beach between West Park and first tower, St Aubin's Bay, Jersey

8 *left:* German sentry at entrance to Town Hall, St Helier, Jersey, 1940

9 *opposite:* The gateway of Morel Farm, Jersey

10 *above:* Fishing nets drying on the churchyard wall at St Brelade's, Jersey

11 *below:* Longueville Manor, Jersey

12 *opposite:* Mont Orgueil Castle and Gardens, Gorey, Jersey
13 *above:* Gorey Harbour, Jersey

14 *above:* Les Halles, St Peter Port, Guernsey
15 *opposite top:* Saumarez Manor, Guernsey
16 *opposite bottom:* Royal Court House, St Peter Port, Guernsey

17 *opposite:* Victor Hugo's statue in Candie Gardens, Guernsey
18 *above:* Alderney: High Street, St Anne
19 *below:* Victoria Street, St Anne

20 Grande Grève, Sark

21 La Seigneurie, Sark, home of the Seigneur, Mr Michael Beaumont

22 *above:* North-west beaches, Herm
23 *below:* Jethou island from the shores of Herm

tomatoes, these are exported in bulk to the British mainland. But this agricultural outlook (an outlook encouraged by the fact that agriculture is still the island's leading industry) does not mean that Guernsey lacks sophistication. It has many fine hotels, and evening activities are well catered for with two cinemas, a theatre, dancing, cabarets, discotheques, and a large choice of restaurants, pubs, and bars.

Despite this, Guernsey retains a peaceful image. It is less crowded than Jersey, and the scenery is generally more beautiful. The cliff walks along the south coast are the best in the Channel Islands, and although the beaches are not as spectacular as the big beaches on Jersey they do have the advantage that, because of the geographical layout of the island, one or more of them is always sheltered whichever way the wind is blowing.

Like the other islands, Guernsey enjoys tax advantages which make shopping a major attraction. The best shops are in the traffic-free streets of St. Peter Port, the island's pretty capital which is built on a hillside above the large harbour and over-looking Herm, Sark and Jethou.

Old St. Peter Port was built around the Town Church, and a stream beside the church used to provide the power for the cottage industries which sprang up in the valley which follows the contour of the Bordage and Fountain Street. Today, long flights of steps still descend these old routes, and they make exploring St. Peter Port a delight, as well as opening up new vistas across the Little Russel to Herm and Jethou.

In the days when St. Peter Port was Guernsey's only possible refuge in case of military attack, Edward III ordered that the town should be walled. It is doubtful whether the wall was ever completed, but in later years granite blocks were set up to mark the town's six gateways, and one of these can be seen to this day outside the post office in Smith Street. A brass plaque on the stone reads: 'This is one of the six stones erected by order of the Royal Court in 1700 to mark the sites of the gates of the town when in the XIVth century St. Peter Port was walled in for defensive purposes.'

For a particularly good bird's eye view of the town, climb up Cornet Street and Hauteville to the top, where the road forks.

KINGS ROAD

KINGS LEISURE CENTRE

ROUTE ISABELLE

STANLEY RD.

ROHAIS

ST. STEPHEN'S C

ROCQUETTES

LES CROUTES

BELMONT ROAD

LES GRAVES

LADIES CO

GI
GRAN
SCH

QUEEN'S ROAD

MOUNT ROW

GOVERNMENT HOUSE

MOUNT HERMON

BROCK ROAD

EBENEZE
CHURCH

MOUNT DURAND

GRANGE ROAD

DOYLE R

VALNORD RD.

VALNORD HILL

LA COUPERDERIE

ST. JOSEPH'S R.C. CHURCH

CORDIER HILL

PRESBYTERIAN CHURCH

ODEON CINEMA

VICTORIA TERRACE

VICTORIA ROAD

NEW PLACE

OUVERT

ISLAND CRAFT CENTRE

CHARROTERIE

PARK STREET

RUE DU PRE

ALLEZ STREET

HAVILLAND ST.

UNION ST.

UPLA

GEORGE

ST. JOHN ST.

ELIZAB
CO

SALEM METHODIST CHURCH

TRINITY CHURCH

MANSELL ST.

BURNT LANE

NOTRE DAME R.C. CHURCH

SAUMAREZ ST.

PRISON

NEW ST.

LE FEBVRE

LES VARGES

HAUTEVILLE

GEORGE RD.

PEDVIN STREET

BORDAGE

MILL STREET

CLIFTON

CONSTITUTION STEPS

BERTHELOT STREET

MAISON HUGO

HAVELET

FOUNTAIN STREET

MARKET STREET

MARKET HALLS

LITTLE THEATRE

ARCADE

HIGH STREET

OZANNE HALLS

CORNET STREET

B.I.A. OFFICE

THE STRAND

B.A. OFFICE

PICQUET HOUSE

TOWN CHURCH

ALBERT PIER

SOUTH ESPLANADE

To CASTLE CORNET

BUS TERMINUS

YACHT MARINA

ALBERT DOCK

OLD HARBOUR
YACHT MARIN

VAL DES TERRES

To BATHING PLACES

HAVELET BAY

ST. P

TOWN O

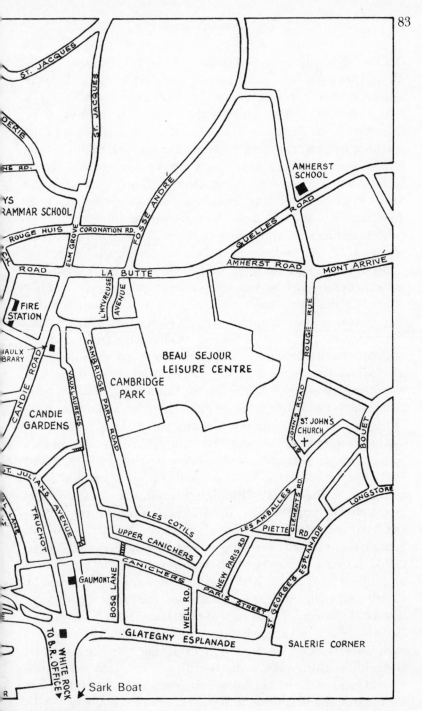

ETER PORT

On the right, between two pillars, is the carriageway of the Montville estate, now public property; and from the carriageway a splendid panorama of the town unfolds beneath you.

St. Peter Port is dominated by the Town Church which is the finest in the area and has been known as 'the Cathedral of the Channel Islands'. Constructed of granite on the harbour's edge, it has been altered continually over the centuries, partly to accommodate the growing population, but also because as the town's dominant building, it was a natural target for attackers. The chancel is thought to be the earliest remaining part of the church, dating from the twelfth century. The portion to the east of this is thirteenth-century, and the south chapel, tower, west door, west end and transepts are fifteenth-century. The steeple was restored in 1721, and after use both as a fortress and as a fire station in the early nineteenth century the present interior arrangements of the church were completed in 1886.

The piers supporting the central tower and the arcading of the nave are particularly noteworthy and along the walls there is a memorial screen to Sir Isaac Brock. The windows are of modern Normandy glass, most of the former stained glass having been shattered by the bombs dropped on the harbour at the beginning of the German Occupation of Guernsey.

At the top of Smith Street is the Court where the island's Parliament meets and where the law courts are held. The island Parliament is called the States of Deliberation, usually referred to simply as 'the States'. Although the majority of its members are elected by popular vote, the States has a constitution different from that of the House of Commons. Membership of the States is made up of 12 conseillers (elected by an electorial college called the States of Election); 33 deputies (elected by voters with a minimum age of 18); 10 douzaine representatives (elected by parish councils); and 2 representatives of the States of Alderney. The H.M. Procureur (Attorney-General) and H.M. Comptroller (Solicitor-General) are members of the States and can take part in debates, but they have no vote. Presiding over the assembly, and with a casting vote, is the Bailiff, appointed by the Crown as civil head of the island, but whose traditional duty is to speak for the island and represent its views to the Crown. The Bailiff also presides over the Royal Court, so a lawyer is always chosen for the post. The Queen's official representative on the island is the Lieutenant Governor of Guernsey. He takes no part in civil or legal administration. The States meet on the last Wednesday of every month except August, and meetings are open to the public. The formalities and voting, carried out in French, underline the Norman origin of the islands. Debates are in English.

In one wing of the Royal Court is the Greffe, or Record Office, where the island's original charters are kept. These charters are the foundation for the special privileges to enable the islanders to fix their own rates of taxation. They also ensure the right to send important exports such as tomatoes, flowers, and the famous breed of Guernsey cattle, to Britain free of duty — a vital factor in the economy of an island which is entirely self-supporting. The charters to be seen in the Greffe, which is open to the public, also lay down the island's military connection with Britain. Guernseymen cannot be called upon for military service outside the island except for 'rescuing their sovereign if he is captured by his enemies, or to reconquer his kingdom if he is dispossessed of it'.

Another old building is the covered market, the French Halles, built as a private venture in 1780. Originally used as a meat market, it was purchased by the States in 1817. When the present meat market was built in 1822, the French Halles was turned over to the sale of dairy produce and fruit from Brittany — hence its name. Just above the French Halles are the Guille-Alles Library and Museum.

Castle Cornet stands like a lone sentinel overlooking the harbour mouth. This ancient fortress, thought to have been built during the reign of Stephen, has played an important part in Guernsey's turbulent history, and has been the scene of numerous battles. During the English Civil War the island supported Cromwell but the Royalist Governor, Sir Peter Osborne, withdrew with a handful of men to Castle Cornet, which they held for nine years. The castle was the last Royalist stronghold to surrender to the forces of Parliament, on 15 December 1651. It was also used by the Germans from 1940-1945, but the War Office formally presented it to the States in 1948 and today it is a peaceful spot. It is floodlit at night during the tourist season.

The castle contains the Royal Guernsey Militia Museum, the Maritime Museum, the Armoury (which includes former uniforms, models and weapons) and an Occupation Museum. On a more peaceful level there is a collection of local water colours by the nineteenth-century artist, Major Peter Le Lièvre, a Guernsey Militiaman. The castle gardens are very fine in late spring.

St. Peter Port's other most interesting building is Hauteville House, the nineteenth-century home of exiled French writer Victor Hugo. Hugo lived in Guernsey from 1855 until 1870, and settled in the house near the top of the steep Hauteville road because from there he could see his beloved France. The house now belongs to the City of Paris and has been preserved as a memorial, complete with Hugo's personal belongings and strangely tasteless yet highly individual furniture just as he left them.

A visit to the house is one of the most fascinating excursions in Guernsey. Hugo, who was born in 1802, was more than just a writer; he was a noteworthy painter, a visionary, an eccentric, and to the Guernseyman of more than a century ago he must have seemed very much larger than life. When he first arrived in Guernsey, a Royalist-turned-republican exile, he stayed in a seafront hotel where Woolworth's store now stands. He moved to a house lower down Hauteville, then with the proceeds of his book of poems, *Les Contemplations,* and an equal sum of borrowed money, he bought what is now Hauteville House. The house had been empty for nine years at that time, because a suicide had taken place there and it was reputed to be haunted by the ghost of a woman. Hugo, a keen spiritualist, did not appear to be bothered by this particular spirit, and he spent two or three years getting the house into what he thought was a suitable shape for his wife and family.

Whether or not his nearest and dearest appreciated his ideas of decoration is not known, but as his wife condoned his installing his mistress, Juliette Drouet, a courtesan with whom he had a 50-year relationship, in a house overlooked by his bedroom window, it may well be that she did not complain about the furnishings.

Hugo, who had a keen eye for a bargain, bought much of his antique furniture from privateers operating from St. Peter Port harbour. In the harbour, too, he acquired hundreds of wooden tea chests, and these he converted into wall panellings and complicated pieces of furniture. He also went in for brightly-coloured porcelain tiles, and was delighted when he obtained one of the pews from Chartres Cathedral. But such oddities are perhaps cancelled out by his Sèvres china service, a gift from Charles X of France. For decoration he chose Chinese wallpaper and valuable tapestries, but he was not averse to hanging on the walls his own signed pen and ink drawings complete with homemade frames.

From the big windows of his rooftop study it is possible to see the French coast on a fine day. Here Hugo, living in spartan conditions and to a strict timetable ('rise at 6, lunch at 10, bed at 10' is inscribed on a dining-room wall), and throwing his scribbled notes on the floor for someone else to pick up and re-write legibly, finished *Les Misérables,* and wrote his famous book *The Toilers of the Sea* about the sturdy island folk among whom he had made his home.

But Hugo left his mark on Guernsey in other ways too. He shared with Napoleon the dream of a united Europe in the days when neither the idea nor the thought of its realisation by peaceful means were popular. He was strongly opposed to capital punishment and fought to save the life of John Charles Tapner who was publicly executed in Guernsey in 1854; when his efforts failed he bought Tapner's death mask and kept it permanently on show. He held spiritualist seances in an attempt to communicate with one of his daughters, who had been drowned, and although he admitted that he had never been able to contact the child, he did claim to have spoken to such diverse characters as Christ, Mohammed, Shakespeare, and Androcles' lion.

On a different level, Hugo was a great humanitarian. He insisted that the many French children on the island should be properly looked after, and paid for them to be provided with a meal of red meat and wine once a week as well as giving each one a useful Christmas present such as a new pair of trousers. He also did much for the poor children of Guernsey, and his memory is revered.

His statue stands in a St. Peter Port park, Candie Gardens, and shows him striding forth in flowing cloak—just as he used to do on his marathon walks around Guernsey. In his last year of exile, Hugo planted an oak tree at Hauteville, predicting that by the time it was fully grown there would be a united Europe. This oak has now become a symbol of European unity and sprigs from it have been planted in many Continental countries. Candie Gardens lie just above St. Peter Port. They are miniature botanic gardens containing a variety of sub-tropical plants, trees and shrubs grown in the open, including a lemon tree bearing fruit that frequently ripens. Within the gardens is the recently completed Guernsey Museum and Art Gallery, which contains many interesting local exhibits. The statue of Queen Victoria, rather more sedate than the one of Victor Hugo, was erected to commemorate her Jubilee in 1897.

Standing high above the town is the red granite column of Victoria Tower, built to commemorate a visit to Guernsey by Queen Victoria in 1846. It replaced an ancient windmill which once stood on the site and from its balcony there are extensive views over the whole of St. Peter Port, most of Guernsey, and the nearby islands. Another landmark on the St. Peter Port skyline is the tower of Elizabeth College, Guernsey's only public school, which was founded in 1563 by Queen Elizabeth I. The school did not really flourish until it was rebuilt in 1826, when '…the boys were regaled in a splendid manner by the workmen with a solid dinner and a hogshead of wine'. Since then it has never looked back. Nearby is the spire of the Anglican Church of St. James the Less, built in 1818 and used for a long time as a garrison church.

In town look out for another military building, the old Picquet House, or guard house, opposite Albert Pier. Built in 1819, it now serves as an excursions office.

Four of Guernsey's principal hotels are in St. Peter Port: Old Government House, The Royal, The Duke of Richmond and La Frégate. All are given the highest grading by the island's tourist authorities, have a full range of services and are open all year. The Old Government House is probably the best known, but the Duke of Richmond has benefited from extensive renovations and modernisation.

Opposite the Duke of Richmond is the island's new leisure centre of Beau Séjour, built in an attempt to attract some of the lucrative conference traffic going to Jersey as well as to provide some much-needed local recreation facilities. The centre was the subject of a great deal of controversy on the Island during its planning and construction, but it has provided such benefits for the visitor as an indoor 'family'-sized swimming pool.

As mentioned earlier, the shopping in St. Peter Port is excellent, and cobbled streets like the Arcades, High Street and The Pollet display an abundance of everything from fresh sea food and country produce to stylish holiday clothes, traditional guernsey sweaters, fine French wines, tobacco, cosmetics, perfume and jewellery.

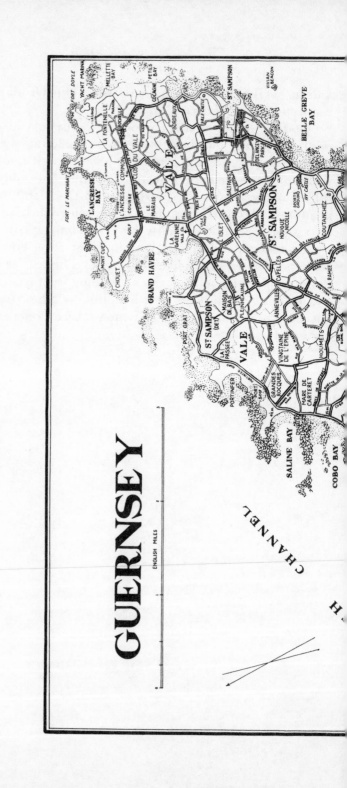

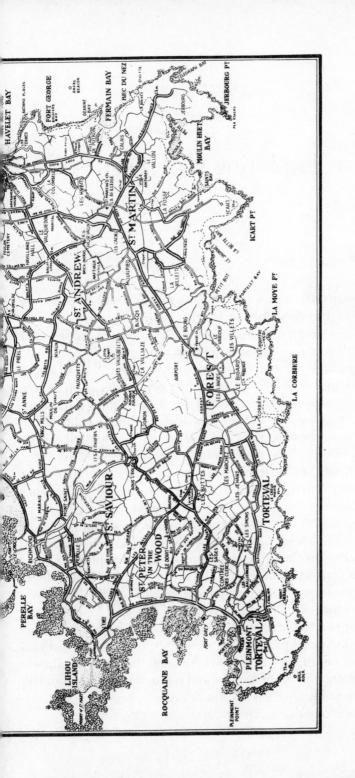

EIGHT

Exploring Guernsey

It was twenty-five years ago, when the summers seemed longer and hotter than they do now, but that year was exceptional even by Channel Island standards. Although we were supposed to be at a youth camp, it was far too warm after about 10 a.m. to do anything except totter from our tents in a quiet corner of a farm in Castel and head for the big, sandy beach that is Cobo Bay. There we swam and sunbathed all day, before going back to the camp site for an evening meal, then catching the bus into St. Peter Port to go to the cinema or to a dance.

Memories are made of such youthful escapades and I have been back to Cobo Bay many times since. The friendly farmer who lent us our camp site is dead, and the extraordinary bridge which some long-forgotten landowner had built to save himself crossing an almost traffic-free road (remarkable because it was the only bridge on the island) has long since tumbled into decay. But the late buses still collect you from the cinema and deposit you back in the far corners of the island, and the tiny village shop in Cobo which sold us our sweets is still there. And, of course, Cobo Bay is still there too—sandy, safe, ideal for all ages, and for my money the finest bay in Guernsey. There are broad stretches of sand, little rocky outcrops for those who want to be alone, and rock pools for the children to explore. Indeed, the bay is dominated by its extraordinary pink rocks, and just to the south of Cobo the rock formation takes on an almost lunar appearance, with one outcrop shaped like a lion and one like a monkey.

There are those who challenge my choice of Cobo as one of

Guernsey's best beaches. But on an island where it is not necessary to visit the same beach twice during a two-week holiday,
there is bound to be plenty of competition. Guernsey has a
glorious variety of beaches, ranging from long sweeping
stretches of sand to small, picturesque coves.

The west coast bays are the biggest. A strong sea wall, built to
withstand the spectacular pounding of the Atlantic during winter
westerly gales, protects the broad plain lying behind the beaches.
The bays have gracefully curving shore lines, and at low tide a
wide expanse of sand and rocks is exposed. The bays are easily
accessible as the main road runs behind them, and as the water
is usually shallow and bathing is safe except where marked,
this is the best area for children.

On each bay, a slipway extends as a paved or cobbled path
across the beach. These were built for the seaweed gatherers so
that they could bring their horse-drawn carts right down on to
the beach. Seaweed gathering used to be a widespread occupation
among the islanders, but the old horse-drawn carts have now dis-
appeared and lorries are used to collect the seaweed — known as
'vraic' — which is used as a fertiliser. During the nineteenth
century seaweed was also used to make iodine, and until recently there were still traces of the industry on Lihou Island off
the west coast. This uninhabited island, reached by a causeway
at low tide, is wild and ruggedly beautiful, with some very fine
rock pools. It once housed a priory, and the remains can still be
seen. Care should be taken not to be cut off on Lihou Island, for
the tide rises quickly and there is no way of getting off except
by waiting for the water to fall again. Facing Lihou is Fort
Saumarez with its Napoleonic Martello tower and a striking
concrete addition built by the Germans during the occupation.

Cobo Bay is more or less at the centre of the west coast. To the
south of it lies Vazon Bay, one of the largest on the island and
consisting of an open expanse of firm sand which is used for
motor racing at times. When the sea is heavy it is also possible to
surf on Vazon, but the bay is exposed to north-westerly winds.
Next to Vazon are rocky Perelle Bay, still used by local fishermen,
and L'Eree Bay. The most southerly bay on this coast, beyond
Lihou Island, is the vast curving shoreline of Rocquaine Bay,

the largest in Guernsey. Within Rocquaine Bay is Portelet, a little harbour formed by a small bay. With its sandy beach sloping gently seawards, Portelet is another paradise for children.

At the south-west corner of Guernsey is Pleinmont Point, where the scenery is wild and romantic. This untamed region is well worth a visit; there is a ruined castle called Pezerie, whose history is lost in the mists of antiquity. The high ground almost opposite gives a good view of this fort, which is built in the shape of a star.

Looking westwards one can see a line of reefs called The Hanois which has been the grave of many ships. In 1862 the Hanois Lighthouse was built, and its revolving beam throws a warning to mariners over a distance of 13 miles. In heavy weather huge seas break around the lighthouse and can be seen clearly from the shore. At the foot of the cliff at Pleinmont Point there is a curious circle of stones with a concentric trench, probably of prehistoric origin. This is called La Table des Pions — 'the footmen's table'.

To the north of Cobo Bay is a series of good beaches: its neighbour Grande Rocques (which is also known as Saline Bay and has a sandy beach); the almost circular and well sheltered Port Soif; pebbly Portinfer; and, towards the north of the island, the massive inlet of Grand Havre below the rugged headland of La Chouet. Running alongside the golf course is Ladies Bay, an attractive sandy beach which seldom becomes crowded. On the northern tip of the island are Pembroke Bay, which has a large sandy beach and is very popular, and its neighbour L'Ancresse, which also has a large sandy beach bordered on three sides by extensive grasslands. Both of these bays are sheltered from easterly winds.

The island's east coast is dominated by the two towns of St. Peter Port and St. Sampson's. Travelling northwards from St. Peter Port the road winds through a rocky wasteland to St. Sampson's, once a prosperous shipbuilding port and later the loading point for shiploads of granite from the Guernsey quarries which flourished there. The harbour is still a commercial port, and the town is always busy. In recent years the local granite industry has revived, and the grey-blue stone is to be seen in buildings all round the island. St. Sampson's is the nearest Guernsey has to an industrial area. It has the only ship repair yard in the Channel Islands, the island's power station, and the Guernsey Tomato Marketing Board's packing station. But St. Sampson's has also developed as an attractive, flourishing shopping centre, although not as comprehensive as St. Peter Port.

Farther north is Bordeaux, a fishing haven in a tiny bay. Then, at the northern tip of the island, is L'Ancresse Bay, with its wide stretch of sand. Behind the bay lies L'Ancresse Common, another pleasure spot for both tourists and local people. Peppered with Martello towers, the common is popular for walks and contains Guernsey's golf course.

Around St. Peter Port and St. Sampson's a number of yacht marinas are springing up, and the fact that these fill up as fast as they are built is evidence of the popularity of these waters. But despite the influx of part-time sailors, the most popular sport in Guernsey must still be walking, and for that it is ideal. Long, unspoiled, and carefully protected cliff paths stretch all the way from St. Peter Port round the south-east and south coasts to Pleinmont.

Visitors can start to follow the cliff paths from the bathing pools at La Vallette. Just past the bathing pools, by the steps leading to Fort George and the start of these cliff paths, is the Guernsey Aquarium. Here, in the setting of a converted German tunnel, are many tanks of curious and colourful local fish.

A winding road, the Val de Terre, leads up to Fort George and St. Martin's, but the footpaths lead to Fermain Bay, a sheltered pebble beach below thickly wooded slopes. The natural beauty of the bay, combined with its proximity to St. Peter Port (there is a summer ferry service) and the fact that it is a morning sun trap, make it one of Guernsey's favourite holiday spots. Cliff walks from Fermain will take you to the fishermen's harbour of Bec du Nez, Marble Bay, and Divette.

The glorious cliff scenery of this part of Guernsey is typical. Perhaps some of the finest scenery is to be found in the south-east corner of the island, the peninsula known as Jerbourg. From St. Martin's Point one can look across Telegraph Bay to the famous line of rocks called the Peastacks. A lane follows the crest of the cliffs, then runs inland to the Doyle Monument. The original monument was erected in memory of Sir John Doyle, Governor of Guernsey at the beginning of the nineteenth century. It was demolished by the Germans, and the present monument was built to replace it in 1953. The panorama visible from the monument includes most of the east coast, the full sweep of Moulin Huet Bay across to Icart Point, and in good weather all the Channel Islands and the coast of France.

A little way from the monument a path leads to Petit Port, one of Guernsey's most popular bays. There is a long flight of steps down but the climb is worthwhile: Petit Port is perfect for bathing.

Next to Petit Port is Moulin Huet (pronounced 'whet') which is easier to get to and therefore more crowded. One route to Moulin Huet is through the 'water lanes', a narrow and steep but pretty path which follows a stream down through a tunnel of trees and ferns.

One of the features of the south coast of Guernsey is these 'water lanes'. They are wooded valleys which follow the course of a stream down to the sea. The shaded paths, rich with luxuriant ferns and other shade-loving plants, make an attractive and quiet route by which to approach some of the nicest beaches. The prettiest and best known of these water lanes is the one leading down to Moulin Huet, but there is also one at Petit Bot.

Saints Bay, the next along the coast from Moulin Huet, is another fine spot for bathing, and the little fishermen's harbour nearby is a paradise for keen swimmers. On the far side of Saints Bay is Icart Point, which gives a fine view of cliffs and bays in either direction. Looking west, you can see La Bette, Le Jaonnet, Petit Bot and Portelet, and in the distance La Moye Point.

The twin bays of Le Jaonnet and La Bette are delightful, with their golden sand and lofty caverns. They are not as easy to reach as some of the other bays so they are often almost deserted even at the height of the tourist season. Petit Bot, next along the coast, makes quite a contrast. This tiny bay, backed by a Martello tower and a café, is very popular, and is approached by two wooded, winding roads which give tantalising glimpses of the golden sand and azure sea. Next to Petit Bot is Portelet, the last sandy bay on this beautiful south coast. It is less frequented than Petit Bot, but harder to get to.

Beyond Portelet the contours of the coast take a wilder turn, and the cliffs have some of the best walks in the island. At Le Gouffre the seething waves boil unceasingly on the rocks. Next comes Corbière Point, then the Havre de Bon Repos, a little bay where at the east end one can find Venus's Pool, a hollow in the rocks which the receding tide leaves filled with clear warm water ideal for bathing. Also on this beautiful stretch of south coast is Creux Mahie, the largest cave in Guernsey. The mouth of the cave is above high water mark, so there is no danger of being cut off.

It is not only the water lanes and the glasshouses which enjoy luxuriant growth. For most of the year, but particularly in late spring and early summer, Guernsey is a mass of flowers. Every mansion and every cottage seems to compete with the public parks in putting on a colourful display. Besides Candie Gardens in St. Peter Port and the flower filled rampart gardens on Castle Cornet, there are fine grounds attached to Guernsey's oldest and best known manor house, Saumarez Manor, in the parish of Castel. Visitors may walk in the grounds beside lily ponds and quaint Japanese summerhouses, and the manor itself has a fine Queen Anne front. Saumarez Park is the setting for Guernsey's Battle of Flowers in late August when brightly decorated floats made of flowers compete for prizes. The 'Battle' is the highlight of a two-day horticultural and agricultural show which attracts more than 20,000 spectators every year. But with such crowds, the old custom of tearing the floats apart and pelting people with blooms has had to be dropped. Instead, the prize-winning exhibits go on floodlit display.

Near Saumarez House is the Guernsey Folk Museum which is full of delightful treasures from the past. The exhibits depict the island's traditional cottage way of life and include old farming equipment, carriages, a cider press and a replica of a Guernsey kitchen complete with spinning wheel and butter churn.

There is also an Occupation Museum at Forest, just behind the Church. This is run by a farmer called Richard Heaume, one of a group of youngsters who have been collecting Second World War souvenirs from the disused tunnels and bunkers on the island since 1956 and who have now formed the island's Occupation Society. The exhibition, beside the Heaume family farm, has some fascinating exhibits which show the deprivation suffered by the islanders during the Occupation when they were forced to make flour from potatoes, jelly from sea moss, tobacco from fig or vine leaves, and gather salt from the sea. Other delicacies of the time include sugar beet syrup, bramble tea, and parsnip coffee. But the museum also shows that the effects of the Occupation were not all bad: one good idea which the Germans had was to number the island's maze of roads — a system which some visitors think could be re-introduced with considerable benefits.

Another relic of the Occupation, the German Underground Hospital, is a popular excursion spot. But in fact the damp, gloomy corridors constructed by slave labour over a three-year period were never used, as the hospital was unfinished at the end of the war.

Nearby is one of the best known sights in Guernsey, the unique Little Chapel at Les Vauxbelets. This is thought to be the smallest church in the world, having room in its 18-feet-by-10-feet expanse for one priest and a congregation of two. It was built beneath the trees beside a former Roman Catholic College, and was the life's work of one of the brothers there, Brother Déodat, who built the framework of concrete then decorated the entire surface, both inside and out, with shells and broken peices of china. In sunshine the resulting effect is a glittering multi-coloured mosaic. After Brother Déodat's death in 1951 the work was completed by Brother Cephas, who used Our Lady of Lourdes as his model. Even now 'contributions' of broken china are still sent from all over the world, but the structure is complete.

Another interesting but rather macabre spot is Bailiff's Cross, a crossroads overlooked by the aptly named Hangman's Inn. A stone with a faint cross cut in it, the Bailiff's Cross Stone, marks the spot where a Bailiff, Gaultier de la Salle, is said to have paused for the sacrament on his way to execution. According to legend, Gaultier de la Salle invented a charge of theft against a neighbour, who was then brought before the Bailiff in court. The neighbour was about to be sentenced when the Bailiff's treachery was discovered and Gaultier de la Salle was forced to change places with the accused, and duly despatched to the gallows not far from this crossroads. The historical story is less romantic; Gaultier de la Salle was sentenced and executed for complicity in the murder of a man who had been pardoned for an accidental killing. He may have halted at Bailiff's Cross.

The Channel Islanders love legends and are incurably superstitious. In Guernsey, for example, there has always been a strong belief in witches, and to this day many granite chimneys have one stone sticking out at an angle from the rest to provide a seat for any passing witch who wishes to stop and warm herself. It is believed that a witch will not curse a house where such a facility is available. Both children and adults who learn of this will be delighted to find a model witch seated on the chimney of the Long'frie Hotel in St. Peter's — it is real enough to give one quite a start at dusk. On a more practical level, the Longfrie provides excellent pub lunches at very reasonable prices.

There are many lovely walks to enjoy inland as well as on the coast, such as the one to St. Saviour's Reservoir which is very attractive in the evening. But if you feel lazy you may prefer to join one of several island coach tours and evening drives organized by local transport companies. The regular bus services, radiating from St. Peter Port, cover the whole island and services are frequent, with the bus drivers always ready to help and advise visitors. The comprehensive pocket timetable is useful.

Of Guernsey's ten parishes, nine have part of their boundary along the coast. The exception is St. Andrew's which, like the southern parishes, has innumerable green and leafy lanes winding between tiny hamlets. The privately run Guernsey zoo at La Villiaze, founded several years ago, has been expanded and improved, but an emphasis has been put on smaller animals which are especially appealing to children.

Quite apart from the church in St. Peter Port, most of the island's churches are attractive and interesting and many of them date from the Norman period. Probably the best known is St. Martin's where, at the gate, there is a prehistoric stone figure known as La Grandmère de Chimquière or, more simply, La Grandmère. The figure used to stand in the churchyard, and the long crack on it is the result of an attack by a former incumbent of the church who was enraged by the presence of a pagan idol. Locals do not pass La Grandmère without saying 'Good morning' to her.

Nearby are two more first class hotels, St. Margaret's Lodge and Ronnie Ronalde's Hotel – the latter owned and run by international television, radio and variety star Ronnie Ronalde.

Vale Church, on the north of the island, which was once almost surrounded by the sea, is nicer than might be expected from its exterior, and includes a Norman chancel which formed part of the original eleventh-century church.

Castel church has another prehistoric figure in the churchyard, but it is far more crudely carved than La Grandmère. Castel church also contains th only wall paintings to be found in Guernsey; they were restored in 1962 and depict from the left the Last Supper, St. Thomas à Becket, and three horsemen encountering three skeletons while out hunting – an illustration of an ancient fable.

Torteval Church has an interesting round tower, and in the churchyard of St. Saviour's is the oldest outdoor monument on the island, to Nicholas Torode who died in 1602. But the oddest church is the parish church of St. Peter-in-the Wood, or St. Pierre du Bois, which has a fine square embattled west tower and a natural slope up towards the chancel which actually rises 4 feet 8 inches. This has given rise to a popular local joke that any bridegroom leaving the church is already going downhill.

Evening entertainment is not nearly as widespread or as sophisticated as in Jersey, and in the absence of pubs (except in town) tends to be centred on the hotels. But there is a big choice of restaurants and sea food is, naturally enough, a speciality. It should be remembered, however, that the island also specialises in agriculture, and Channel Island milk, cream and butter are all first class. A unique souvenir of Guernsey is a traditional Guernsey milk can, sold in every size ranging from a 24-gallon can to one suitable for fixing to a charm bracelet. The globular cans, topped by a narrow neck, were styled so as to use the least possible amount of metal and prevent spillage. They have a tight-fitting lid to keep out the dust.

NINE

Alderney

You have to walk right round the whitewashed sundial outside Alderney airport to read the homely inscription carved on it: 'Do as the sundial does—count the bright hours only'.

There are plenty of bright hours on Alderney, which is the third largest of the Channel Islands in spite of being only three and a half miles long and one and a half miles wide. Sunshine and clean air combine to give a sparkle to this rocky and faintly untidy island, whose 1,700 inhabitants have decided, somewhat reluctantly, that the empty beaches and windswept headlands deserve a wider audience and have therefore set about trying to build up a small tourist industry. The effort often appears very half-hearted. 'Don't write too much about us', one official begged after I had made a fact-finding visit to the island. 'We don't want too many people coming here'.

That opinion is supported by many of the islanders, almost all of them comparative newcomers themselves, and they are slow to accept visitors. Yet the island does now have a holiday industry, albeit still a very small one, and there is a welcome of sorts.

The skylarks will probably greet you first, bursting with song as you wait for the taxi to take you the few hundred yards from the tiny airport with its grass runway (can it be true that incoming pilots line up their light aircraft on a white-painted stone in a nearby lane?) to St. Anne, the island's capital and only town. Or perhaps your welcome will be from the gulls, screaming over the huge harbour as you step ashore from the hydrofoil or fishing boat which has carried you from neighbouring Guernsey. And, even if the islanders are not exactly pleased to see you, there will be further greetings as soon as you set foot on the cobbled streets of St. Anne, for this 'town' has village manners, and everybody still says 'Good morning' to everybody else.

Alderney, only eight miles off the coast of France, was once a smugglers' paradise, and the general air of prosperity coupled with an apparent lack of industry makes one wonder if old habits die hard. But Alderney, totally evacuated in the German Occupation during the Second World War, and still littered with concrete gun emplacements which cannot be dismantled without blowing up the entire island, has in fact worked hard to re-establish itself by rather more legal methods.

The island's name comes from the Norman-French Aurigny or Origny, a name immortalised in Macaulay's poem 'The Spanish Armada', for it was from 'Aurigny's Isle' that news was signalled to the English Fleet of the arrival of Spanish ships in the Channel. The places where those historic beacons were lit are still known as Les Béguines.

The central part of the island is in the form of a plateau 250-300 feet above sea level, and is made up of farmland and the tiny airport. In the south and south-west this plateau ends dramatically in cliffs, towering over the sea; on the northern, eastern and south-eastern sides the land slopes gradually towards rocky and sandy bays, where bathing is delightful and usually safe.

Alderney was once known as the Cinderella of the Channel Islands—and as far as tourism is concerned it looked for a long time as though the island might continue to qualify for that title. Sea services between Alderney and the rest of the Channel Islands, let alone the British mainland, are poor, although there is a summer hydrofoil link with France. But in recent years, thanks to the operations of the island's 'own' airline, Aurigny, flying little Islander and Trislander planes which do not need a great deal of room to land or take-off, and in which passengers sit close behind the pilot, thousands of holidaymakers have been introduced to the island and to its attractions as a place where one can really 'get away from it all'. The air services to South-

ALDERNEY

BURHOU
Bird Sanctuary

The Swinge

Fort Clonque

Clonque Bay

Airport

ST. ANNE

Harbour

Brave

Save Bay

Camping
Area

Longy Bay

N

—— Roads

SCALE:- 3/4" to approx. 1175 yds

ampton, France, and the other islands have also made Alderney, with its low rates of taxation, a haven for businessmen.

The island's main drawback is that it was not particularly beautiful in the first place, and what natural attributes it did possess have been marred through the ages by the structure of forts and gun emplacements as Britons, French, and latterly Germans have all recognised its strategic importance overlooking the Channel approaches. But it does have a peace and charm which, since the end of the war, has encouraged many British people to 'emigrate' to the island—a movement spurred, no doubt, both by the tax advantages of such a move and the fact that at the time of writing Alderney is the last of the Channel Islands on which it is still financially or legally possible for an 'outsider' to buy or build a reasonably-priced house. These 'new' islanders tend to be possessive about Alderney and clannish in their social life. 'Our attitude', one newcomer with a military past confessed to me with disarming honesty, 'is: "Pull up the ladder, Jack; I'm all right".'

Fortunately, there are plenty of exceptions to this philosophy, and on my first visit to the island I was shown around by a friendly local publican, Drew McQueen—an introductory tour which included several refreshment stops and which culminated in a magnificent lunch at The Albert House Inn in St. Anne. On other occasions islanders have gone out of their way to invite me to their homes, an experience which many visitors also report. And when a local hotel reneged on an off-season booking (not as rare an experience on Alderney as one might hope), an embarrassed local tourism official put me up at his home. These are the sort of incidents which make one warm to Alderney and wish to return there again and again. Incidentally, I am glad to report that the hotel in question has now been closed down.

Alderney's history has been more violent, and more chequered, than any of its neighbours. In 1338, during the Hundred Years War, it was captured and looted by the French. Settlers from Guernsey rejuvenated the island in the fifteenth century.

The activities of pirates in the Channel, preying upon merchant ships, and the persistent French threat, led to a British decision during the reign of Henry VIII to build a fort on

Alderney overlooking the harbour at Longy. But work was never completed, and the structure was demolished in the 1840s to make way for the building now known as Fort Essex. This name was given to the new building because it was thought that the original castle had been built by the Earl of Essex, the favourite of Queen Elizabeth I, who was executed for treason in 1601; but records show that the work was begun and abandoned some years before the Earl of Essex was born.

International politics and military strategy left another mark on the island in the 1840s, when France's development of a powerful naval base at Cherbourg alarmed the Admiralty, and a scheme was dreamt up to turn Alderney into the 'Gibraltar of the Channel'. It was necessary to build a major harbour on the island, and in 1844 approval was given for the construction of a breakwater to screen Braye Bay from the Atlantic and provide a big, sheltered anchorage. The 4,680-feet breakwater was begun in 1847 and finally completed in 1864. A second breakwater, running north-west from Roselle Point was also planned, but this was never begun. A chain of ten forts, stretching from Fort Clonque in the west all along the north coast as far as Fort Essex on the south-east, was also constructed between 1845 and 1861.

But within six months two huge holes were torn in the breakwater by winter gales, and although these were quickly repaired there was repeated winter damage to the breakwater, which faced the full force of the Atlantic. By the end of the nineteenth century the breakwater was considered obsolete, and the damaged end was removed—an operation which reduced the wall to its present length of 2,850 feet. This breakwater was still enough to shelter the commercial harbour from all but the strongest north-easterly gales. The abandoned end of the wall now forms a 600-yard sunken reef, a hazard which forces shipping to make a wide turn into the harbour. And although it is not much more than half its original length, the breakwater still dominates the island and gives Alderney the appearance of having a huge handle on one side—a peculiarity which makes the island easily distinguishable from the air.

During the Second World War Alderney suffered further deprivation and ugly additions, undergoing hardships which have affected it to this day. It was evacuated, then occupied by the Germans who turned it into a fortress. Russian prisoners of war and French Jewish political prisoners were used as slave labour to build massive gun emplacements and defensive works, together with a network of underground shelters and tunnels. A memorial to these slave workers, with tablets in French, Russian and Hebrew, stands at the point where the road to Mannez Quarry forks to Saye Bay, above which one of the slave camps was situated. It is a sad and evocative spot, reminding one of the horrors and despair this island must have witnessed and of man's continuing cruelty to man.

The famous Alderney breed of cattle was almost wiped out by the Occupation, but Guernseymen evacuated sufficient beasts to retain a herd which was re-established on Alderney after the war.

The Germans officially surrendered Alderney on 16. May 1945, but when the first islanders returned six months later they found their houses damaged or destroyed and most of their possessions missing. In addition, nearly all the island records had vanished.

Until the end of 1948 Alderney was administered with the help of British Home Office officials, and the economy of the island was maintained by heavy rehabilitation expenditure on the part of the British Government. Agriculture was re-established, the States and Court were modernised so that the last vestiges of feudalism were swept away, and it was agreed that Guernsey should assume responsibility for some aspects of Alderney's government. But the island is still under-populated, and new residents are allowed to settle there—although this is done under strict controls to prevent spoliation of the island's peace and character. To this day housing and hotel development is severely restricted.

Because of these interruptions to its development and history, Alderney now has a very different character to the other Channel Islands. It is far more British in outlook than its neighbours, and English is the island language. Its residents are predominantly settlers of middle-age, with independent means, and many of them have adopted what almost amounts to a uniform of navy-blue guernsey oiled wool sweater, navy blue slacks, and yachting shoes.

The original islanders are hard to find, and the old Alderney version of the Channel Islands' Norman-French patois has almost died out. The patois is now spoken and understood by fewer than half-a-dozen islanders, and as most of these are old the language may well vanish soon. There is not even any incentive to pass it on to new generations for, as one of the remaining patois speakers told me, it is necessary to go across to the Breton ports, where the fishermen still speak and understand a similar dialect, if you want to chat with anyone in patois.

Like the language, many of Alderney's other old customs have become lost in the mists of antiquity. Suspicions that the ancient custom of smuggling is still rife linger, and are even encouraged (as a joke, you will be assured) by the islanders. It is not quite apparent who is supposed to be smuggling what, and to whom.

One custom which has been saved, and revived, is 'Milk-a-Punch Sunday', observed on the first Sunday in May. The origins of this unique custom are obscure, but it is thought that at one time it was permissible to milk anyone's cow and take an egg from under anyone's hen on that day to make up the punch. Today most Alderney bars offer regular customers a free glass of rum and milk punch on Milk-a-Punch Sunday.

Unusually for the Channel Islands, the capital—and only town—of St. Anne is situated in the centre of the island. Three-quarters of Alderney's population lives in St. Anne, with its narrow cobbled streets and predominance of early Victorian buildings.

On summer mornings the main street, Victoria Street, a pedestrian precinct during the day, becomes jammed with shoppers as people buy their groceries or window-gaze outside the sprinkling of modern-ish boutiques. In the other streets a solitary traffic warden moves cars on and attempts vainly to enforce the town's somewhat superfluous one-way traffic scheme (superfluous because by lunch-time the two streets concerned are almost deserted while, as I know to my cost, the traffic warden's vigilance continues). Movement in general is hampered by the fact that everybody knows everybody else, and people stop every few yards to pass the time of day with a friend or neighbour.

St. Anne's Parish Church, with an imposing granite archway and wrought-iron gates at the entrance to the churchyard, is the town's—and the island's—most distinctive building. It is built mainly of stone quarried on Alderney, and was consecrated in 1850. During the German Occupation it was used as a store and suffered a great deal of damage, and its six bells were removed; but it has been carefully restored by the islanders and the bells were found in Cherbourg and rehung.

The parish church replaced a former church, the sixteenth-century clock tower of which still stands near Marais Square, in the oldest part of the town. A stream used to run through the square, where St. Anne's housewives gathered to do their washing. But now the square is cobbled and—thanks to the work of the German Occupation forces who left the island at least one worthwhile asset by tapping two underground reservoirs—every home has running water.

Not far from the bottom end of Victoria Street a short hill leads off to The Butes, a windswept recreation ground with extensive views down to Braye Harbour and across to the busy Channel shipping lanes beyond. The Grand Hotel on The Butes is by far the best hotel on Alderney—an island where much of the accommodation seems somewhat claustrophobic (although there is some good self-catering accommodation available, particularly the charming estate of log cabins known as Palm Springs, if you book early enough). Ray Parkin, who runs both the Grand Hotel and Palm Springs, has the distinction of being one of the more enlightened people on Alderney when it comes to tourism.

But apart from in these places, accommodation can be hard to find—although if you are lucky, prices are low. Eating out can be a problem too, but the Albert House Inn in Victoria Street does huge and very appetizing bar lunches. On the other side of the road, the Georgian House Hotel restaurant is the nearest that Alderney gets to a really first class restaurant.

At the opposite end of town to The Butes are the old Court House, where the States of Alderney meet, and the peaceful

Royal Connaught Square with its smattering of fine buildings including the former Government House (now a community centre) and the old-established Royal Connaught Hotel. Another open space nearby, Le Huret, is where the island's farmers used to meet to decide when to gather and share out the 'vraic', or seaweed, used as a fertiliser. Almost opposite the Rose and Crown is the island museum, which has some particularly interesting social exhibits as well as relics of the German Occupation and a comprehensive record of the many shipwrecks in the area.

Alderney has many beautiful beaches, most of them excellent for children—but swimmers should beware of strong undertows and other currents at some spots. The Harbour area is within easy walking distance of St. Anne; for the others you will need to walk, hire a car or bicycle, or catch the school bus which occasionally visits some bays to set down or pick up passengers.

Braye Bay is close to St. Anne and includes Braye Harbour. At low tide there is a magnificent sweep of rock-free silver sand, and bathing is safe at all times. Along the coast, to the west of the Harbour, with good views of Burhou and Little Burhou, are Crabby and Platte Saline Bays. In Crabby Bay there is good deep-water bathing from the rocks below Fort Doyle. Platte Saline is a fine gravel beach, but there is a strong undertow and swimming can be dangerous.

On the north-east coast, Corbelets, Arch, and Saye Bays have fine stretches of firm sand and are ideal for children. The bathing at Saye (or, as the locals say, Soye) is the best in the island.

On the south-east coast, the large, sandy expanse of Longy Bay is also excellent for children, with good shrimping and prawning among the rocks. The only Roman building in the Channel Islands, known as the Nunnery and dating from the fourth century, is on the shore, and Essex and Raz forts are at either end of the bay.

Finally, at the south-western end of the island, there is Telegraph Bay, which is well worth the walk by the cliff road. The steps to the beach are steep, and as a result of cliff falls they can be dangerous too. The persistent will find a beach of fine sand, surrounded by rocks and caves. But visitors should be very care-

ful not to get cut off by the rising tide, for the steps are inaccessible after half-tide.

Apart from bathing, the most popular sports on the island
are cricket and football, which are played on The Butes, and
golf on the 9-hole course overlooking Braye and Longy Bays.
There is sailing from the harbour, but beyond the breakwater
these are dangerous waters and even the most experienced
yachtsmen should heed local advice. Horses can be hired at
Verdun Farm, in Longy Road, and there are tennis courts at
the Grand Hotel.

But the visitor to Alderney is seldom looking for entertainment. Alderney is essentially an island for the walker, the camper
(you can camp at Saye Farm), or for those who are simply looking for peace and quiet.

One of the best ways of exploring the island is by hired bicycle.
You can get advice at the airport, or in town, about hiring and
it is only fair to add that demand for bicycles is such that the
machine you hire for £1 a day may not have a resale value of
much more than that. But hills are gentle, and one can get great
enjoyment from exploring an island which, having been rav-
ished by history, now seems to be left to its own devices. Walkers
should note that footpaths are not always safe (watch out for
German dugouts and barbed wire) and are often over private
land—although landowners rarely bother walkers.

The complete circuit of the island is the most challenging walk,
but it is better split up into easy sections.

The north and west coasts can be covered in a couple of easy
and interesting walks from St. Anne. First go down to Braye
Harbour, and turn left along the main road past Crabby Bay,
the lake formed by the disused York Hill Quarry, Fort Doyle,
and the sweep of Saline Bay, where German gun emplacements
have been imaginatively converted into unique summer houses
or beach huts by islanders who hire them for a nominal rent.
West of Saline Bay are Fort Tourgis, the rocky expanse of
Clonque Bay, and Fort Clonque, which is one of the more picturesque of these military monuments. The indented 'Devil's Chair'
rock at Clonque Bay is said to be haunted by a monk tied there to
drown by wreckers whom he caught at work; the ghost appears

in the 'chair' when there is to be a shipwreck on the island.

Above Fort Clonque the aptly-named Zig-Zag Path climbs steeply up the heights of The Giffoine, an overgrown hillside thick with gorse and heather hiding many quiet picnic spots and with splendid views. At the top of the Zig-Zag Path a road leads west to the cliffs above Hannaine Bay and the sea-battered Les Etacs, or Garden Rocks. From here the energetic can reach Trois Vaux Bay, the Tête de Judemarre headland, and Telegraph Bay.

By now you have worked your way round to the southern coast, and a footpath and road lead back past the airport to St. Anne. The rest of this half of the island can be covered in the same walk or separately — starting out at the top of the track leading down to Telegraph Bay and continuing on the road round at the 'back' of the airfield.

A natural rock 'chair' at Val de l'Emauve is the setting for a romantic legend concerning the daughter of a former Seigneur of the island and her lover, a farmer's son, who used to meet at the chair in defiance of the Seigneur's orders. Rather than face enforced separation when they were discovered there together, the couple are said to have joined hands and jumped into the sea where they were drowned. Although the road turns inland at Platte Cotil, the cliff paths can be followed farther east past Val du Sud and Val de Fret, and spur roads leading into town can be picked up at several points along the route.

The airport, which one rounds on both these walks, is worth a visit. Although it is such a tiny spot, it is seen by the islanders as a centre of communication, and some even call in there occasionally for a cup of tea at the little snack counter.

East of St. Anne the island is flatter, with Longy Road running across the spine of the island to Longy Common. Any of the spur roads leading south off Longy Road will take you back towards the south-coast cliff path. This path continues east, past a big natural rock arch and above accessible beaches (where bathing can be dangerous) to the Hanging Rock — a 50-feet spur of rock sticking out from the cliff face which Alderney legend claims is the 'hook' from which Guernsey tried to tow Alderney away — and the sixteenth-century Essex Castle, now restored and used as flats. The castle guards the entrance to Longy Bay, once the main harbour of the island. The other side of the bay is formed by Raz Island, with its partially-ruined fort, and the causeway leading to the island.

The far north-east of the island is skirted by the coast road which passes Fort Houmet Herbe, Fort Quesnard, and the Quesnard lighthouse—the latter dates from 1912 and can be visited. The road runs between the lighthouse and Mannez Quarry (from which the island's only 'railway' runs back to Braye Harbour) to Fort Corbelet, Corbelets Bay, and neighbouring Arch Bay. There are moves to restore and reopen the railway, now the only one on the Channel Islands.

Beyond the headland and Château à L'Etoc (now a private house) is the horseshoe-shaped Saye Bay, backed by sand dunes and a good place for picnics. A footpath leads up to the next headland, guarded by Fort Albert, or one can take the road back to the Memorial to the victims of the German Occupation, and so to town.

The sweep of the north coast at the back of Braye Bay is worth exploring on its own, for it is a quiet and strangely evocative part of the island. Walkers can quench their thirst, or get a snack, in a harbourside pub—although Braye Harbour is not the most salubrious corner of Alderney. Better, perhaps, to return to St. Anne, with its selection of coffee shops, bars, pubs and restaurants where prices are still a pleasant surprise.

Alderney shares with the other Channel Islands the attraction of cheap drinks, cigarettes, and luxury goods because of the lack of V.A.T. and other taxes. There is also a better-than-average chance of good weather. What the island does not have is big crowds or a swinging night-life—but then that is exactly what the people who go there are trying to avoid.

Alderney's nearest neighbours, apart from France, are Burhou and the Casquets. Burhou is separated from Alderney by a dangerous channel known as The Swinge, which is lined with rocks and has a vicious tide. The group of rocky islets known as the Casquets are about seven miles to the west of Alderney, and have been the scene of many wrecks, including that of the passenger ship *Stella* in 1899, when many died. The rocks used to be marked by fires which were kept burning continuously, and the first lighthouse on the Casquets was erected in 1790.

Fact and fiction about these dramatic and dangerous rocks combine in Swinburne's poem 'Les Casquettes'; the girl in the poem actually lived on the rocks, and it is said that she was once induced to visit relations in Alderney—and didn't like it. 'The world' as she called Alderney, was too full of trouble and noise—and she hurried back to her lonely rocks.

TEN

Sark

Sark—far more of a 'pearl set in a silver sea' than England could ever be—is more than just one of the Channel Islands and more than the last feudal community of Europe too; it is a world of its own. It has somehow managed to retain its unspoilt atmosphere and its extraordinary individuality despite the wars and battles which have raged around it for the past 1,500 years—a process which can be likened to the stopping of time itself.

Sark, fourth largest of the Channel Islands, lies eight miles east of Guernsey and there is a daily boat service from St. Peter Port except when the sea is too rough. It is three and a half miles long, about a mile wide, and consists almost entirely of a 300-feet-high central plateau from which valleys run steeply down to the sea. Because of this the sea is usually in sight, and yet far below you—a fact which helps to give the island its other-worldly atmosphere because somehow you feel as though you are up on a table high above the rest of the world and living in a world which is complete in itself. The rocky coast, with its soaring cliffs, is deeply indented all round Sark, giving a fairly small·island the surprising total of 40 miles of coastline. Yet, always contradictory, Sark has only four miles of road, none of it metalled, and a population of only about 500.

Roads are not needed, because Sark has no motor vehicles. Visitors to the island must travel by hired horse-drawn buggy, by bicycle, or on foot. The occasional tractor can be seen working in the fields or ferrying visitors' luggage to one or other of the island's hotels; but that is all.

In a way, Sark is an island of negatives. It has no income tax, no death duties, no adoption laws and no divorce. What it does have is a feudal constitution dating back to the reign of Queen Elizabeth I. It has a hereditary ruler, the Seigneur, who today is Mr. Michael Beaumont, a former aero engineer and grandson of the famous Dame of Sark, Sibyl Hathaway, who refused to leave her island during the Occupation and treated the invading Germans with an unexpected mixture of haughtiness and contempt.

The government of the island is the Court of Chief Pleas, a feudal body which legislates on local matters. It is made up of the Seigneur, the Sénéschal (judge or president), the Prévôt (sheriff), the Greffier (clerk), the Constables, the island's 40 tenants, and 12 elected deputies. This Parliament meets three times a year at Michaelmas, Christmas, and Easter in the Sark Boys' School building, and although the Seigneur can veto any decision that it makes this is very rare. The Sénéschal also has his own court for the granting of licences and for dealing with minor offences. He has the power to impose a fine or to imprison offenders in the island's two-man jail for a maximum of two days. The tiny airless granite jail is one of the tourist sights on Sark and is thought to be one of the smallest prisons in the world. It looks extremely uncomfortable, which is perhaps why it is very seldom used.

Sark is, in fact, the smallest state in Europe, but as far as democracy is concerned it has turned its back on its neighbours and the islanders show every sign of liking it that way. They raise no objection to the fact that the Seigneur retains a number of feudal rights, among them the fact that he is the only person on the island allowed to keep pigeons (an ancient rule designed to protect the seed corn) and the only person on the island allowed to keep a bitch. Mr. Beaumont, who is in his mid-forties, says: 'I like to retain old customs. They are quite harmless, and once they lapse they will have lapsed for ever'. One custom that he does not retain, however, is the ancient feudal *droit de Seigneur* under which a bride had to spend her first night as a married woman with the Seigneur rather than with her husband. Mr. Beaumont is anxious to assure those interested that in failing

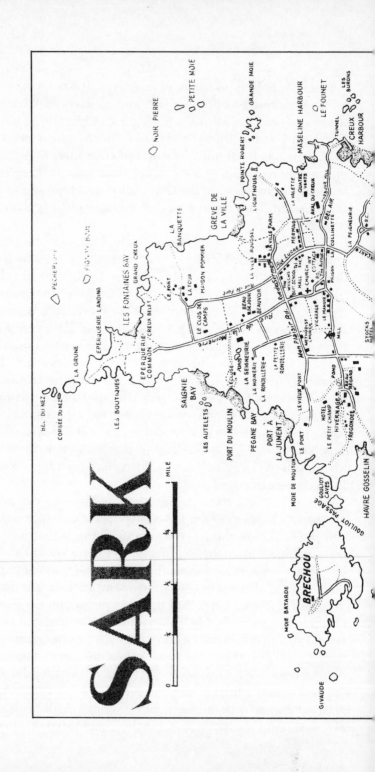

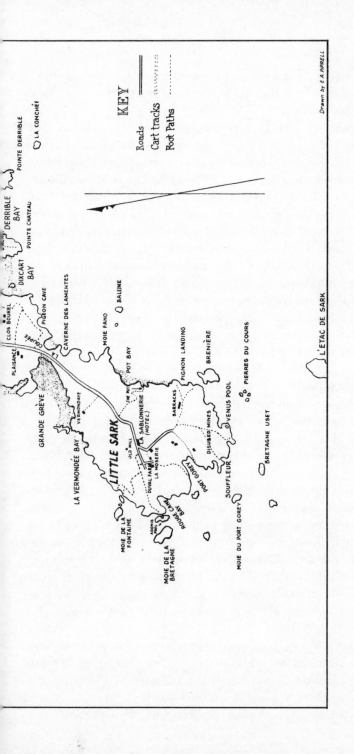

POINTE DERRIBLE

DERRIBLE BAY

POINTE CHATEAU

DIXCART BAY

CLOS BOUREL

PLAISANCE

PIGEON CAVE

COUPÉE

GRANDE GRÈVE

CAVERNE DES LAMENTES

LA CONCHÉE

MOIE FANO

BALINE

LA VERMONDÉE BAY

VERMONDAYE

LITTLE SARK

OLD MILL

POT BAY

IN RUE

PIGNON LANDING

BRENIÈRE

LA SABLONNERIE (HOTEL)

BARRACKS

LA MOSERIE

DUVAL FARM

PORT GOREY

DISUSED MINES

VENUS POOL

PIERRES DU COURS

SOUFFLEUR

MOIE DE LA FONTAINE

ADONIS POOL

ROUGE CANE BAY

BRETAGNE USET

MOIE DE LA BRETAGNE

MOIE DU PORT GOREY

L'ÉTAC DE SARK

KEY

Roads
Cart tracks
Foot Paths

Drawn by E. A. PIPRELL

to enforce this right he is making a concession to the niceties of modern manners rather than casting any reflection on Sark's budding womanhood.

In a more modern vein, the Seigneur also bans all aircraft, including helicopters, so the only way to reach Sark is by sea. Both the ferry from Guernsey and the occasional seasonal hydrofoil services land at the new La Maseline Harbour, on the east coast of the island. The islanders raised £52,000 to build this deep-water harbour and it was opened by the Duke of Edinburgh in 1949. Two rock tunnels link it with the adjacent Creux Harbour, a very sheltered harbour for fishing boats which is exceptionally well protected from the elements but which suffers from the handicap of being probably the smallest harbour in the world. In northerly gales, when La Maseline Harbour is unusable, ships have to use the sheltered waters of the oldest harbour of all, Havre Gosselin, on the other side of the island and under the lee of Brecqhou Island just off the coast of Sark. Ships cannot tie up in Havre Gosselin and passengers have to be ferried ashore.

From La Maseline Harbour and Creux Harbour, a steep path known as Harbour Hill climbs up to the village and on a summery day one quickly regrets the lack of transport. More than 70,000 visitors a year, the vast majority of them day-trippers, toil up the hill, but the people of Sark are unrepentant. Even the island's doctor has to do his rounds on a bicycle and the local ambulance is drawn by a tractor.

Refreshments are available at the top of the hill, and there too you will find touts anxious to hire you a bicycle for £2 a week or £1 a day. Alternatively visitors might like to hire a horse-drawn taxi (about £8 a day) which comes complete with a highly individualistic driver and island guide; but there are only 35 of these so an early decision or advance booking are essential.

Regrets over the absence of adequate transport are short-lived; Sark is a peaceful island, and without any background traffic noise one quickly finds oneself listening to the birdsong or to the lapping of the waves on the rocks far below.

The two most popular excursions on Sark are to the Seigneur's house, La Seigneurie, and to the precipitous path known as La Coupée which divides Sark from the peninsula known as Little Sark. Walking across La Coupée one realises that at some time in the not too distant future Sark will become two islands, for the 260-feet-high path is a sliver of soft rock and clay which is now only 10-feet-wide in places. It has long been a matter of local conjecture just how long the path will remain in place, and every winter gale brings new fears. But, for the present, La Coupée is still there, a picturesque spot which is particularly dramatic in rough weather when the spray from the waves 260 feet below can fall on the path as heavily as rain. La Coupée is also said to be haunted by a headless dog and the devil's coffin. Local tradition says you must jump over the coffin, but gives no instructions about the dog. At La Coupée it is possible to climb down to the beach, Grande Grève, on the west side. You can swim at Grande Grève.

The Seigneurie dates from 1565, but its antecedents go much farther back than that into the very beginning of Sark's history. There are no traces of Neolithic settlement on the island and although the Romans are known to have landed there they do not seem to have stayed for very long. But in 565 St. Magloire, a Welshman, and 65 monks formed a monastery there, near what is now the Seigneurie. A portion of one of the walls of the monastery can still be seen in the grounds of the Seigneurie. The monks wanted only to work and worship in peace on the island, but they were harassed by marauding Vikings and other raiders, and even when William the Conqueror gave the island to Mont St. Michel in 1042 it could not be adequately protected. Sark became something of a pawn in the struggle between England and France and on one occasion, according to Sir Walter Raleigh, it was recovered from the French only by the ruse of landing British troops disguised as a funeral party and carrying their weapons hidden in a coffin.

King Edward III finally lost it in payment of a debt, and as pirate raids continued the monks quit the island for good in 1412. Sark was abandoned.

But in 1558, a Jersey nobleman, Helier de Carteret, decided to live on Sark and to develop it. In 1565 Queen Elizabeth I recognised the wish of de Carteret and his followers to develop the island and granted him a Charter to rule the island as Seigneur on the understanding that he would colonise it with forty men, each armed with a musket.

This Charter established the number of families which should live on the island as tenants, and that number remains good to this day. The properties descend from father to son or to the eldest daughter, and the original allotments cannot be divided, left to somebody else, merged or sold without the approval of the Seigneur who has an option to buy the allotment himself and must also approve any prospective purchaser. Land reverts to the Seigneur if the owner dies without a suitable heir, but this has happened only once in the island's history. The Seigneur himself can sell the island and all its rights but only by consent of the reigning sovereign.

Although de Carteret re-established the island as a going concern, he did not establish a dynasty. The position of Seigneur passed from hand to hand, until a renegade privateer called John Allaire, operating out of Jersey and Jethou, became rich enough to buy for his daughter, Mary, the title of Dame of Sark. Mary married a Guernseyman, Thomas Guerin Collings, whose grand-daughter was Sibyl Hathaway.

Mrs. Hathaway, perhaps the most famous figure in the island's history, married an American called Bob Hathaway in 1929. Despite their adventures with the Germans during the Second World War, the Hathaways afterwards brought a great deal of publicity to the island and the film *Appointment with Venus,* which was set in Sark, helped to restore the island to the prominence it had enjoyed between the wars as a tourist attraction.

Today it is possible to stay at the Seigneurie, for the Seigneur lets flats at the back of the house; but prices are high. The pretty Italian-style walled gardens are entered through an arch fitted with fine wrought-iron gates which the people of Sark gave to the Hathaways as a wedding present. The gardens are open to the public twice a week (Monday and Wednesday).

There are comparatively few accessible beaches in Sark, but two of the best are close to the harbour. A footpath off the Val du Creux round the cliffs to the left leads to the first of these:

Derrible Bay. Behind the bay is the awe-inspiring cave, Creux Derrible. A headland known as the Hog's Back divides Derrible Bay from the wooded glen leading down to the Dixcart Bay, with its natural rock arch; one of the nicest spots on Sark. The two main hotels on Sark, the Dixcart Hotel and Stock's Hotel, are a short distance above Dixcart Bay and do good meals as well as providing accommodation.

Two of the most famous spots on Little Sark are the sea water pools known as Venus's Bath and the Pool of Adonis—both popular with swimmers but both about one and a half hours' walk from La Maseline Harbour. The pools, which the sea leaves filled with crystal-clear water, are marked on local maps, but are still hard to find and many visitors miss them altogether. For Venus's Bath cross the Coupée and follow the road past the Old Fort, turn left off the main road by some cottages, turn left again up the first lane, and head towards the remains of the old mine shafts. You will eventually come on to a grassy track which leads to the Pool, right opposite the rock out at sea known as L'Etac. Venus's Bath is almost circular, about 20-feet deep, and above the tide level for about five hours. The smaller and less attractive pool nearby is called Cupid's Bath.

The Pool of Adonis is on the other side of Little Sark, and to reach it you keep on the main road from the Coupée, turning right before the last cottage. Turn left at the fields towards the gorse, where you will pick up a path bearing south-west, in the direction of Guernsey, to the clifftop. The pool is in the rocks opposite the southern end of a rocky offshore islet called Moie de la Bretagne, but it is a hard scramble down to it and it can only be reached at around low tide. The sheer-sided pool is deeper than Venus's Bath, but the water is just as clear and inviting.

On Sark itself there is lots to see, and the day-tripper will either have to return, or else make a decision about what to leave out. There are a number of fine caves, among them the so-called Victor Hugo's Cave at Havre Gosselin (which is said to have inspired the famous French author's novel *The Toilers of the Sea*), which can be reached only by sea; 'Gulls Chapel' at Grève de la Ville; 'the Chimney' at L'Eperquerie; and the 'Fairy

Grotto' with its huge natural arch at Les Fontaines. Facing Havre Gosselin are the Gouliot Caves which include the famous 'Anemone Cave' in which can be found masses of anemones in red, pink, green and yellow, as well as the rare white anemone. Other interesting zoological specimens such as sponges can be found in the cave, which is best reached by boat although it is possible to wade in at low tide.

Another interesting visit is to the site of the silver mines at Port Gorey. Some of the shafts are still to be seen, and it is worth noting that about 35,000 ounces of silver were extracted from them during a twenty-year period before the entrepreneur responsible went bankrupt.

The village in the centre of Sark is the highest in the Channel Islands: 365 feet above sea level. It is roughly triangular in shape, and surrounds St. Peter's Church which dates from 1820 and whose bell was cast from guns formerly used by the Sark militia. There is a handful of houses, a post office, café, modern art gallery, and a smattering of shopkeepers including one special-ising in locally-made jewellery. At Rue de Moulin is the old windmill, a distinctive building which has no sails and which was decapitated by the Germans during the Occupation and used as a lookout point. It has since been restored.

A worthwhile walk or bicycle ride is to Point Robert and the lighthouse, towering above the harbour (it is possible for visitors to be shown round, except on Sundays). The steep cliffs in this part of the island are dangerous, even where paths are marked.

Perhaps because it is so different to the other Channel Islands—or indeed to anywhere else in the world—Sark enjoys a popularity, particularly among day-trippers, which its attrac-tions do not always warrant. Contrary to some people's ex-pectations there is no entertainment or tourist facilities. In the words of the Seigneur: 'There is nothing to do on Sark unless you like walking, beautiful scenery, or swimming in cold water'. But that does not prevent a constant demand for accommodation on the island, so advance booking is essential for anyone intending to stay there.

And once there, the visitor will either be bored stiff or else completely enraptured by the peaceful atmosphere. It is an at-

mosphere where old beliefs and old customs die hard. As in
Guernsey, there is a strong belief in witchcraft and no islander
would build a house without a witch's seat on the chimney. When
a wedding takes place the bride and bridegroom must travel
round Sark dispensing cake and wine, and when there is a death
on the island members of the deceased's family must call at every
house to give news of the event. Graves are always dug to the
exact shape of the coffin. And when tiny clay pipes are found
that date from Sir Walter Raleigh's governorship of Jersey, when
tobacco was introduced to the islands, the people of Sark will tell
you that they are 'fairy pipes' which belong to the *pouque
layes*—the 'little people'. Put out fresh milk for the *pouque layes* to
drink, so the island farm folk tell you, and they will do things for
you in return; things like finishing your knitting, or finding
some small item which you have lost. But, like Tinkerbell in *Peter
Pan*, the *pouque layes* have little time for disbelievers and will
inflict their own particular form of punishment on those who
make them angry: they will stop your hens laying, or get the
blackberries to scratch you, or—worst of all—they will make you
add up wrongly.

And part of the magic of Sark is that, somehow, few visitors
will end up scratched, or with their sums all wrong. For on this
enchanted island it is easy to believe in the 'little people'—or
for that matter in practically anything else.

ELEVEN

Herm, Jethou and the other islets

They call him 'King Peter', and it would be fair to say that Major Peter Wood does not exactly object to that title. He is, to all intents and purposes, the king of the small, centrally-situated Channel Island of Herm; the man who decides what happens there and, when it comes to it, who visits the island. The latter point is an important one because Herm is everybody's dream island—a favourite playground both for the people of neighbouring Guernsey and for approximately 100,000 visitors from the British mainland and from overseas, almost all of them day-trippers, who go there every year.

They find King Peter a kindly and hospitable monarch; a man who has achieved the impossible. The ex-Army officer who once told a newspaper reporter that he had leased Herm because he thought there was going to be a nuclear war, and he did not believe that anyone would bother to bomb the Channel Islands, has not turned Herm into an eccentric's hideaway. On the contrary: he has brought up a family of six children there, turned the island into a thriving business, done all that in the full public gaze, and achieved his ambitions without spoiling Herm at all.

The latter is the most important point as far as the rest of the world is concerned. Herm, three miles off the east coast of Guernsey and right opposite Guernsey's capital of St. Peter Port, seems to embody everything that an island should be. It is roughly one and a half miles long and half a mile wide, has some of the best beaches in the Channel Islands, yet also manages

HERM

Alderney Point

Mouisonniere Beach

Pierre
aux
Rats
(obelisk)

Shell Beach

The Bear's Beach

N

Fisherman's Beach

Belvoir Bay

Farm

Caquorobert

Harbour   VILLAGE

**Little Seagull
Main Camping Area**

White House Hotel

Rosaire Steps

Le Creux Pigeon

Pt. Sauzebourge

———— Tracks   - - - - - Footpaths   SCALE :– 3/4" to approx. 350 yds to contain a wealth of pretty scenery, some fine cliff walks, a big common where rabbits scamper practically between your feet, and a cluster of tiny cottages and shops which make up an embryo village built around an absurdly small harbour.

During the summer a stream of launches make the twenty-minute crossing from St. Peter Port to Herm, ferrying trippers to and fro. In winter, visitors intending to stay at the White House Hotel, the only hotel on Herm and just around the corner from the harbour, are met by a special launch service, and there are also daily ferries carrying food and other essentials to the island on what is known as the 'milk run'. So the island is not cut off from the rest of the world, even though it manages to convey that impression.

If the tide is right, visitors step ashore on Herm at the harbour, its jetty and crane somehow contriving to look like children's models. Alternatively, at low water the ferries have to use a jetty known as La Rosière Steps, which juts out into a stretch of water called the Blue Lagoon a few hundred yards south of Herm harbour. Once ashore you walk; there are no cars, or even roads, on Herm — although you may get a lift along the dusty tracks between the ferns on a passing tractor.

Clustered around the harbour are the Mermaid Tavern, which serves as a snack bar, tea garden and island pub, and a handful of boutiques and gift shops in a little shopping piazza. This Continental-style piazza was the cause of some controversy when Major Wood started building it a few years ago, with many visitors fearing that it would spoil the island's atmosphere. This sort of complaint is one of the hazards if you happen to own an island like Herm; after a while visitors start to feel that, even if they don't actually own the island, they do have some sort of stake in it. And one of the nice things about 'King Peter' is that he understands, and even sympathises, with these feelings. He listened dutifully to all the complaints — mine among them — but then went ahead with his plan just the same. I am glad, if somewhat mortified, to report that the finished piazza fits happily into the island's surroundings.

Above the 'village' a path climbs steeply up through woodland to the backbone of the island, past the eighteenth-century Manor

House, which was once the home of Sir Compton Mackenzie, and a group of farm cottages and down to Belvoir Bay, an attractive and very sheltered sandy beach on the east coast of the island which many visitors head for almost automatically. You cannot get lost: Herm is dotted with neat little signposts pointing you in the direction of its various attractions.

Although the chief of these attractions are its beaches, Herm is an island which is fun to explore. Footpaths encircle the island, winding their way through ferns and pinewoods, across farmland, and around the high cliffs which dominate its southern tip. It is too small for children to wander far, and too compact to tire the elderly. It is an ideal excursion centre for visitors from Guernsey, but outside the main season it is ideal for getaway-from-it holidays as well. Standards at the White House Hotel are fairly high, but so are the prices, a fact which does not seem to be reflected in the demand for rooms. Intending visitors need to book early. Incidentally, the hotel also has a good restaurant. But, rather than staying at the hotel, a personal choice would be the self-catering accommodation now being developed on the island, particularly in the old farm buildings above the harbour which are undergoing some imaginative conversion.

Nature has been kind to Herm. The clear air, without a trace of pollution, and the warm sunshine mean that flowers and plants grow in abundance. On sheltered lawns the daffodils bloom early, trumpeting the arrival of spring long before it touches the British mainland; and in summer, in the hedgerows, wild foxgloves tower higher than a man. All this helps to give the island a fairytale atmosphere—an atmosphere enhanced by the very names given (on an island where there is not much else to name) to the fields: Moulinet, Bon Jour, Pan, Valley Panto, Big Seagull, Little Seagull, Fairy Rings, Bramble, and Monku.

The southern part of the island is split by sheltered valleys where the vegetation is particularly lush and where cottages nestle. For the most part, these cottages are inhabited by the hand-picked residents of Herm—the people, most of them from the mainland, who make up the island's workforce. On one January morning I met a middle-aged northern factory worker busy painting the snack bar on Belvoir Bay. He wore overalls and an open-necked shirt, and a sun which seemed to be gaining rapidly in strength blazed down on him. I asked him why he had moved from Manchester, to an island where his pay was probably no more than adequate and his prospects nil. He smiled and pointed up at the sky. 'Where else in the British Isles', he asked, 'would I be painting outdoors in January?' And he contentedly resumed his work.

Behind Belvoir Bay, a popular suntrap protected from all but easterly winds and excellent for swimming, a track leads between the fields and along the spine of the island — dropping down to the vast stretch of the Shell Beach which is, from the sea or from the air, one of the landmarks of the Channel Islands. The half-mile long beach looks from a distance as though it is of golden sand, but in fact it is made up of countless millions of shells most of which have been ground down to a fine powder. The enthusiast may still find plenty of complete specimens though, many of them from such faraway places as the Caribbean. The shells are deposited on this promontory by the ubiquitous Gulf Stream, an arm of which touches Herm at his point. Again, the beach is fine for sunbathing and swimming, although it is much more exposed than Belvoir Bay and shelves a little more sharply.

Backing on to the Shell Beach is Herm Common, a deserted stretch of land which makes up the northern quarter of the island and which is inhabited only by grazing cattle and by whole families of rabbits. The Common is dominated by a stone obelisk known as Pierre aux Rats, built there a century ago after fishermen had complained about the removal of an older obelisk which they used as a navigational marker. The twin hills of Le Petit Monceau and Le Grand Monceau form the southern boundary of the common, and their lower slopes were once a Neolithic burial ground. Indeed, the entire northern part of the island is of considerable archaeological and historical interest, for there are numerous cromlechs and stone circles there and bones and pottery fragments dating back to prehistoric times have been unearthed. It is thought that this part of Herm may once have been a burial ground not only for people from neighbouring Guernsey, but also from the coast of Normandy. Major Wood's charming wife, Jenny, a sensible yet sensitive woman, says that the Common has a strangely haunted air, as if great emotions have been aroused there at some time which still linger to charge the atmosphere. Mrs. Wood is not alone in feeling this, for many visitors to the island have gone away with a similar impression of the Common.

The Woods are a fascinating and extremely hospitable family — Major Wood being a New Zealander who was reared on a sheep farm in North Island before moving to Wiltshire as a teenager, and his wife coming from a village in the West Riding of Yorkshire. Both feel satisfied and fulfilled by their achievement in turning Herm into a cross between an unusual but comfortable home, a successful farm (Major Wood's herd of pedigree Guernsey cattle is the largest in the Channel Islands), and a thriving holiday island. Jenny Wood has told her story graphically in her book *Herm: Our Island Home*; Peter Wood is perhaps best described by his wife, who says that he is a combination of realist and visionary.

They live in a beautifully appointed house called the Seigneurie, with views across to Guernsey and carefully tended sheltered gardens. But it is a home which they found by accident. They had lived on the island for two weeks before one of the tenants invited them to visit his home, which he said was called Lady Perry's Cottage. Jenny Wood recalls: 'We'd never heard of it, much less seen it. We followed him up the hill and then, to our surprise, he turned along the arched passageway beside the keep and proceeded to pick his way through the rubbish and undergrowth beyond. We followed him down a single track, breasting our way through high grass and a tangle of bramble and briar until we came to a faded blue door in a high granite wall. We passed through it and found ourselves in a vast walled garden'.

The tenant in question was leaving Herm within two months, so the Woods moved in. A great deal of work had to be done on both the house and the gardens—the latter including a strange round tower on a promontory which was marked on Admiralty charts as 'the old Mill of Herm'.

As the renovation of the house progressed, and the family increased, and the island developed into a thriving industry with a growing population, the Woods faced other problems. A nursery school had to be established for the seven or eight youngsters. It was a school with a difference, for the accent was on outdoor activities, but it developed into a full-scale primary school and formal lessons must have been successful too, for all the pupils passed on to secondary education on Guernsey or on the mainland with flying colours.

Island industries have changed with the years. Farming and tourism take pride of place, but the islanders have also turned their hands successfully to making shell souvenirs, weaving, and other cottage industries. With such tasks playing an important part in the island's economy, particularly during the winter months, the Woods have always had to choose their 'subjects', or tenants, with care, and if they have sometimes seemed autocratic that is because a good mix was and is essential.

Besides the Manor House and the White House Hotel, Herm's most interesting building is perhaps St. Tugual's Chapel. This Spanish-style chapel adjoins the Seigneurie, and was unfurnished and unused when the Woods found it. The history of the chapel is not clear. Indeed, it is not even clear quite who St. Tugual was—although she is popularly supposed to have been a Welsh woman murdered by the Saxons. There is thought to have been a chapel on the site since the sixth century, and the Woods have brought the present building (complete with tiny bell tower opposite the entrance) back to life even though it has not been officially consecrated. It now has seating for 36 people, and Major Wood takes morning services there most Sundays. That a handful of worshippers can still make themselves sweetly heard is indicated by the fact that when a press party visited the island and were liberally entertained, one of them had to spend Saturday night in the cottage next to the Chapel. He awoke next morning suffering from the effects of Herm hospitality to the sound of angelic singing—and rushed from the cottage shouting that he was dead. He discovered morning service in full swing at St. Tugual's.

Perhaps such a thing could happen only on Herm, an island

where realism can be elusive. But it is a wonderfully away-from-it-all holiday spot and, despite its compactness, there is plenty of scope for exploring. The Common is bounded by beautiful beaches, and although the shore is rather rocky on the western, or Guernsey, side of the island the north-facing Mouissonnière Beach is empty and unspoilt—deserted by the day-trippers in favour of the Shell Beach and Belvoir Bay. Indeed, Mouissonnière has been used for filming in high season for this very reason, but if two or three people do turn up there and form a 'crowd', there are always empty coves among the rocks opposite Guernsey, although you may have to clamber briefly through the bracken to reach them. Sunbathers, who should always be wary in the Channel Islands, should however take particular care on Herm: the very clear air and the cool breezes off the sea usually make the strength of the sun deceiving.

The southern half of the island is ringed by cliffs, and although it is possible to clamber down to the sea in places the only really worthwhile bathing is at Belvoir Bay. A footpath from Belvoir goes right round the southern tip of the island to La Rosière Steps on the opposite coast, and following it makes a bracing, interesting and scenic walk.

And in the evenings...well, there is always the Mermaid Tavern. This focal point of the harbourside 'village' doubles up as snack bar and tea-room during the day; but after the launches and the day-trippers have gone back to Guernsey, and only the islanders and the overnight visitors remain, it reverts to the more familiar type of tavern and is the scene of some lively evenings.

If there is a drawback to Herm, it is the shortage of holiday accommodation. And that, of course, is just the way it should be. The island will undoubtedly retain its popularity, and attract even more visitors in the future, as 'King' Peter's eldest son, Simon Wood, takes over the running of Herm's tourism and extends the range of self-catering accommodation. But one cannot imagine that Herm will ever become crowded, or brash, or 'touristy', if only because the Woods will not permit such a thing to happen to what is, after all, their home.

Even if there are a few more residential holidaymakers in the future, Herm will never be spoiled, and it will never be like any other holiday island. As if to prove that very point, the regulars at the Mermaid Tavern will tell you of the island's most frequent visitor, a ghostly monk in a dark brown habit who has been seen in the Chapel, in the grounds of the White House Hotel, and at other spots on Herm. A clairvoyant who visited the island identified the monk as Pierre du Pont, who lived on the island in the eleventh century and was burned at the stake during a massacre. If that bears any relation to the truth, it is yet another indication of Herm's faintly horrific past. But one cannot feel apprehensive or frightened on such a lovely island where nature has been so generous and the people are so nice. As if to echo this, the islanders will rush to reassure you about their monk. He is, they say solemnly, a very friendly ghost.

A narrow channel separates Herm from its small, circular, conical-shaped neighbour, Jethou. Unlike Herm, Jethou is the property of the Crown and is leased to private tenants. At the time of writing the tenant is Sir Charles Hayward, the elderly Chairman of the Trustees of the Hayward Foundation, a charitable trust, who retired there in search of peace and quiet. As a result of this, Jethou does not welcome visitors and it is not possible to visit the island without special permission which has to be sought beforehand. Anyone landing on the island without this permission will quickly be asked to leave, and although many visitors to the Channel Islands would undoubtedly like to include Jethou in their travels the tenant's wishes are, in fact, respected and adhered to by the Channel Islanders themselves.

Jethou is a rocky island, about one and a quarter miles in diameter and three miles off the east coast of Guernsey. It once belonged to the Abbey of Mont St. Michel, in neighbouring France, but for centuries no-one lived there and Guernseymen used to visit it only to hunt rabbits and to raid the many wrecks which ended up on the island or its surrounding rocks. Pirates were executed on the island, and it also seems to have been the haunt of smugglers—a fact which may account for the large number of hidden banknotes found during renovations to a house on Jethou at the end of the nineteenth century.

One of the island's tenants during this period was a brandy

smuggler called Lieutenant Fielding, who enhanced the Channel Islands' reputation for both eccentricity and lawlessness by getting his workers to fire at people in passing boats.

About fifty years ago the island was leased to Sir Compton Mackenzie, who did much of his writing there. Later, in 1934, the island passed to an American, Harold Fortington, who took to Jethou the first car ever seen there. Since the 1930s the island has seldom been open to visitors.

Above the landing place at Crevichon, where there is good bathing, is Fairy Wood, a mass of bluebells in the spring. There is also good bathing on the east and west coasts, or from a tiny sheltered cove on the south facing Grande Fauçonnière Rock. Close to the sandy Fauçonnière Beach is an enlarged natural rock-pool called Puffin's Pool which is good for swimming, and there is also a remarkable 'creux' or blow-hole, known as Devil's Hole. Myriads of seabirds occupy the island and the rocks offshore, among them the pretty puffin.

One can make the circuit of the island by the one and a quarter-mile-long lower path or climb to Jethou's 267-feet highest point. Otherwise there is nothing to do. The most impressive building is the Manor House, which has a spacious garden containing a mulberry tree thought to be 250 years old. Building on the site of the Manor House dates from 1717 but the present building has been extensively altered.

The remaining islands in the Channel Islands group include Burhou, off Alderney; Lihou, whch is linked to Guernsey at low tide; and Brecqhou, just off Sark.

Burhou is a long, low, green island about one and a half miles off the coast of Alderney opposite Fort Tourgis. Although it is nearly a mile long and up to 200 yards wide, it is uninhabited for most of the year and is now a bird sanctuary. There are the ruins of an old stone house on the island, but bird watchers are advised to provide their own shelter. Local boatmen will take visitors to the island where there is a large puffin colony — a fact which has led Alderney people to call Burhou the Isle of Puffins.

Brecqhou, a mere forty yards off Sark, is the only island for which the freehold ever becomes available, and its present owner, banker and businessman Len Matchan, lives on the 160-acre island in some comfort. He travels between Brecqhou, London and Jersey by helicopter, and this machine has become a familiar sight in the area. He has built a special landing pad for the helicopter on Brecqhou, and says: 'Travelling by air and car I can be in my office in London in two hours five minutes'. Thus the Channel Islands are jerked rudely into the commuter belt. Mr. Matchan finds Brecqhou the ideal place for thinking and planning. He lives alone except for staff, although friends often stay in one of the four cottages adjoining his home. 'People can get to Brecqhou only in my boat or my helicopter', he says. 'The great thing about an island is that you only have people you want there'.

The tiny islands of Les Ecréhous lie about seven miles east of Jersey and eight miles off the French coast. They can be visited from Jersey by anyone who can persuade a boatman to go there, but access excepted there are no problems because they are officially part of Jersey. Three of the islets have houses on them; Maître Ile, which is privately-owned and is kept as a bird sanctuary; Blanc Ile; and Marmotière. In fact, Marmotière has ten houses, and perhaps the world's smallest street. At low tide thousands of rocks and pools are revealed, and in the last century Les Ecréhous were once the home of a sailor called Philip Pinel, who spent forty years alone there and was known locally as the King of the Ecréhous. Today the islands are uninhabited in winter, but in summer they are popular with visiting yachtsmen and a Custom House has been built to deter people from taking the obvious opportunities that exist for dealing in contraband.

The larger but more scattered group of islets known as Les Minquiers lies about twelve miles south of St. Helier but only one, Maîtresse, is inhabited. At low tide the islets cover about 80 square miles, but this shrinks to almost nothing at high water. The islets are used mainly by fishermen, and although they officially belong to Jersey the French flag can sometimes be seen flying there—a Breton protest against the International Court of Justice's ruling on the ownership of the islands after the Second World War.

Finally, there are the Chausey Islands, a group of about 300 islets—many of them no more than rocks— 28 miles south of

Jersey and only about eight miles off the coast of France. Although the group is part of the Channel Islands, they come under French jurisdiction. Only one of the islands, Grand Ile, is inhabited—it has a tiny farm, an inn, a post office, a lighthouse and an old fort—but although it is an ideal excursion spot, the fishermen living there do not make any special attempt to welcome visitors and it is only the occasional yachtsman from Jersey who finds his way there.

General Index

138

GUERNSEY